I'm Right,
You're Wrong,
Now What?

I'm Right, You're Wrong, Now What?

BREAK THE IMPASSE
AND GET
WHAT YOU NEED

Xavier Amador, Ph.D.

HYPERION   NEW YORK

Library of Congress Cataloging-in-Publication Data is available upon request.

ISBN: 978-1-4013-0346-4

Hyperion books are available for special promotions, premiums, or corporate training.
For details contact Michael Rentas, Proprietary Markets,
Hyperion, 77 West 66th Street, 12th floor, New York, New York 10023,
or call 212-456-0133.

Design by Victoria Hartman

FIRST EDITION

1   3   5   7   9   10   8   6   4   2

For Bob
Who is always faithful.
Come home soon.

AUTHOR'S NOTE

With only one exception—involving a transcript from a television documentary I participated in—I have used aliases and changed certain biographical facts and other elements to protect the identities of the persons who appear in this book. In many instances I have created composites to further protect privacy and to better underscore certain points I was making. Unless stated otherwise, when I write about a conversation I personally had I am relying on my memory, and in some instances notes, and acknowledge that some factual errors are inevitable. Nevertheless, I have sought to faithfully represent the issues and conversations in every instance.

ACKNOWLEDGMENTS

First and foremost I am very grateful to the thousands of people who participated in LEAP seminars over the years. Through your comments, your challenges, the problems you posed, and the role plays we did with one another you taught me much I could not have learned any other way. For that reason, and because many of you asked that I write it, this book is also yours. Although your name is not on the cover, know that this book could never have been written without you.

Thanks also to Brenda Copeland and her colleagues at Hyperion for their immediate and ongoing enthusiasm for this book. As my good friend Stephen King so aptly said "To write is human, to edit is divine." Thanks, Brenda, for making this a much better book than it would have been without you. By the way, I don't actually know Stephen King, but what he said about editors, like many things he writes, rings so true I feel we know each other well. Brenda helped my writing ring truer, and for any writer there are few greater gifts.

Special thanks to Steve and Barbara Delinsky for strongly encouraging me to meet Susan Ginsberg at Writer's House. You were right! Thanks, Susan, for your faith, support, and advice. You did much more than help me with this book—you also helped me to think about where I am headed as an author. I look forward to going there together.

Many people have either read earlier versions of the manuscript and given me feedback, shared their stories, argued with me because they cared, or supported the work in other ways. They include Henry Amador; Maria Cristina Bielefeld; Gerry Spence; Jayme and Dylan Mackay; Mary Beth Polek; Liz and Tom Brondolo; Bob Leahy; Jim, Yvgette; Noah, and Thomas Mina; Hilda Speicher; Bruce Hubbard; Sandra and Marcela Davila; Rachel McCoy; Elizabeth Pappadopolous; Lisa Hunter; Jason Savage; Dave Schaich; Angela Noncarrow; Judy Kern, Les Pockwell; Emily Saladino; and Bethany Strout.

If my mind has slipped and I left anyone out that should have been thanked, I know it will come back to me after the book goes to press! I will thank you in person then, and hope you are not offended, because although your name may have slipped my mind it never left my heart.

CONTENTS

INTRODUCTION

I failed the test.

I knew I would, because I froze when I read the first question. My vision narrowed, the classroom darkened, the pencil kept threatening to slip out of my sweaty fingers, and the test questions all turned into hieroglyphics. I knew in that horrible moment that I would fail the final statistics exam—or as I called it, "sadistics." I was doomed and should have left the room right then. The only reason I didn't was that David, the teaching assistant who was proctoring the test, and had been my statistics tutor for two years, had faith in me, and my high grades up until then had proved him right.

"I have bad news for you," David said two days later when he found me in the New York University clinic where we both saw patients. "Let's go into one of the therapy rooms and talk."

I almost laughed at his choice of venues for giving me the bad news, but I didn't. Instead, I said, "I know. I failed the final."

"I was really surprised," he said kindly. "You understood the material. What happened?"

"I had a panic attack. I froze."

David suggested I call Professor Cohen, explain what had happened, and ask to take the exam again that same day. He even phoned ahead and put in a good word for me, so with a glimmer of hope I made the call.

"Hello," the gruff baritone voice said.

"Dr. Cohen, it's Xavier Amador. I believe David told you I was going to call," I said quickly, a little short of breath for some reason.

"Yes, yes, he told me, but I don't know what I can do for you. I've never allowed anyone to retake the final. It's unprecedented."

"Can I tell you what happened before you make a final decision?"

"David already told me," the professor said impatiently, "but if you insist, go ahead." I reminded him of my previous grades and told him of my little problem—now a very large one—with math anxiety. He was a psychologist, so I was hopeful my confession might elicit some sympathy. Then I delivered what I felt was my most compelling argument for being allowed to retake the exam.

"If I fail your class, I'll have to pay tuition again and wait an entire year before I am awarded my Ph.D. That seems like a very high price to pay for failing this one last exam. I've passed all the others for two years now."

"Sorry, but I can't set a precedent like this. If I do it for you I will have to do it for everyone."

"But I'll be delayed an entire year! I already have a job offer at Columbia University and I'll have to turn that down," I pleaded, my voice cracking.

"I'm not unsympathetic, but it would set a precedent and I can't do it."

"But you can. It's your decision!"

"No, I can't."

"But I'm sure you can. I checked it out with—"

"I have to go now," the professor interrupted. "I'm sorry. I wish you the best of luck." He had stopped listening and the call ended at an impasse. He would be submitting final grades in two weeks and my fate would be sealed unless, I thought, I could convince him I was right and he was wrong. As you will soon see, I didn't exactly convince him he was wrong, but I did persuade him to let me take the test again.

Whether the issues are big or small, we all get into these situations every day. We know we're right and the other person is wrong. The problem is that the other person also knows he's right and you're the one who's too stubborn to admit it. Such impasses occur at home, at work, at school, and elsewhere. The specifics and scope of the situation may change, but the underlying dynamics do not. And what have you done up until now to make the person you were arguing with see things your way? Delivered a rational argument? Tried to make him feel guilty? Sulked? Yelled? Threatened? Has it worked? Have you gotten what you wanted? More important—have you gotten what you actually needed?

If you've focused myopically on getting your opponent to say, "You're right, I'm wrong," which is what we all think we want during the heat of battle, I'd venture to guess that nine times out of ten you haven't gotten what you needed and the times you have won were usually at the expense of the relationship.

Until you start to do something different and begin to focus on what you actually need—getting the person to do the thing you want him to do—those outcomes are going to remain the same.

What's at risk may be as important as whether or not your kid drops out of college, whether or not your aging parent goes into a nursing home, or whether or not you and your partners sell your business. Or it may be one of the countless everyday impasses you reach while trying to negotiate smaller matters, such as whether or not you really did promise your wife to take the family to the beach next weekend when you had planned to play golf with your brother, or whether your health insurer will pay for the nuclear stress test your doctor recommended.

One thing all these disagreements have in common—the one you may not even have considered—is that you have to create a positive relationship with that other person if you're ever going to get what you need. You have to turn him from an *adversary* you're arguing with into a *partner* who is working with you. It doesn't matter if that other person is your coworker, your bank manager, your child, or your spouse. It may be for five minutes or five days, or it may be for the rest of your life, but right then, at that moment, you need that other person to work with you instead of against you. And to accomplish that you have to show some genuine interest in his perspective and his needs.

In my seminars on how to break an impasse I always ask, "Why would anyone want to listen to you if he felt you had not first listened to him? Quid pro quo." This important psychological principle—which is the cornerstone of my method for breaking an impasse—is far from new. More than two thousand years ago the Roman poet Publilius Syrus said, "We are interested in others when they are interested in us." Psychologists who are expert in conflict resolution and marriage and family therapy have written about this fundamental principle for decades. Dale Carnegie, the author of the seventy-year-old best-seller *How to Win Friends and Influence People*, writes, "Philosophers have been speculating on the rules of human relations for thousands of years, and out of all that speculation, there has evolved only one important precept. It is not new. It is as old as history. Zoroaster taught it to his followers in Persia twenty-five hundred years ago. Confucius preached it in China twenty-four centuries ago . . . Jesus taught it among the stony hills of Judea nineteen centuries ago. Jesus summed it up in one thought—probably the most important rule in the world: 'Do unto others as you would have others do unto you.'"

We are interested in others when they are interested in us.

More recently the authors of *Getting to Yes, The 7 Habits of Highly Effective People, Good to Great, How to Argue and Win Every Time*, and other insightful observers of human relations have all emphasized this same fundamental principle of persuasion. But despite the ancient lineage and popular dissemination of this simple and logical truth, it is too often overlooked when we are lured into an "I'm right, you're wrong" situation and end up thrashing around like a fish caught on the end of a line, certain that if we just try hard enough (speak more loudly or repeat our position once again) we will win. Sometimes we do succeed in bending the other person to our will, but not without doing some damage.

Relationships Are the Key

Whether at home or in the workplace, when relationships are damaged—when trust is lost and anger simmers—bad things happen. Healthy relationships among colleagues and between suppliers and clients are central to business. Without them no business can exist, much less turn a profit. And, believe it or not, preserving the health of your relationships can even help to keep you alive. The results of a recent study of 3,682 couples, published in the journal *Psychosomatic Medicine*, found that women who give up and give in during arguments with their husbands are four times more likely to die prematurely than women who argue productively. The women who held it in also had a higher risk of depression and irritable bowel syndrome. The study's authors conclude that healthy arguments are good for your health and longevity. I couldn't agree more.

One of my most vivid memories of the frustration—and futility—that comes with trying to argue with someone when I *knew* I was right and he was wrong took place more than twenty years ago. It is also an embarrassing reminder of how I used to reflexively turn a deaf ear, all the while demanding that I be heard. My brother Henry had just come home after his first psychiatric hospitalization for a serious mental illness. Medication had brought him back to reality, but within a day of his homecoming I found that he'd tossed his bottle of pills in the garbage. Naturally, I asked him why he'd thrown it out. The conversation went something like this.

"I'm okay now," he explained. "I don't need those pills anymore."

Since this was exactly the opposite of what he'd been told in the hospital, I made a point of reminding him. "But the doctor told you that you're probably going to have to be on this medicine for the rest of your life. You can't just stop taking it."

"He didn't say that."

"Yes, he did. I was at the family meeting, remember?"

"No, he said I had to take it while I was *in* the hospital."

"Then why did he give you that bottle of pills to take home with you?"

"That was just in case I got sick again. I'm fine now."

"That's ridiculous! That's not what he said."

"Yes, it is."

"Why are you being so stubborn? You know I'm right."

"It's none of your business."

"When you got sick it became my business. And besides, I'm worried about you."

"I don't want to talk about it. Just leave me alone."

And with that he walked away. Unfortunately, I was right, and within two months he relapsed and returned to the hospital.

As anyone can see (even though I didn't at the time), my "I'm right, you're wrong" approach to resolving that disagreement wasn't going anywhere. All it did was spark an argument, make us both angry, and cause us to dig our heels in deeper. My brother wasn't listening to me. And why should he, since I wasn't listening to him? I was too busy insisting on the correctness of my point of view. Even worse, however, the "I'm right, you're wrong" approach threatened to destroy any trust we might have had in one another and with it our relationship, and without a trusting relationship, I would never get what I needed.

After that first argument—and predictable impasse—I did not suddenly remember the wise advice I quoted above, rejoice at the insight, and stop badgering my brother with my point of view. Instead, I took the bait over and over again until our relationship looked like a battered and bloodied fish slapping the ground in its death throes. It seemed like every time we tried to talk about this issue it ended the same way and worse. He became suspicious of my motives, and I became more certain he was being stubborn and immature. Once we had been close and could talk about anything, but now we were like two bulls locking horns whenever we tried to spend time together because one or both of us would always manage to bring up the medication issue. Predictably, we became distant and began to avoid one another. This impasse lasted nearly five years! But all that changed after I stumbled upon the techniques I will share with you in this book. Using these tools I was able to turn our adversarial relationship into—once again—a close partnership that gave me the leverage I needed to convince him to take the medicine.

Despite this early success I wasn't always able to reproduce this result in other situations—impasses I encountered in my professional and personal life—because I did not have an easy-to-remember outline, or road map, I could rely on. I knew the techniques but didn't always know when to use them or how to apply them systematically.

It took me ten more years to devise a reliable method out of this kind of impasse, a road map for nearly any disagreement—really for human relations—that I call the Listen-Empathize-Agree-Partner method, or LEAP.

The purpose of LEAP is not to get your opponent—and that is what he's become when you're at an impasse—to agree that you are right and he is wrong. The goal is to get him to agree to do whatever you need him to do. That may sound like a contradiction, but it's not. If you are like most people, you lose sight of what you really need whenever you take the bait and end at an impasse. Whenever we focus on the narrow issue of who's right we lose sight of the bigger picture: the specific thing we want the other person to do, the health of the relationship, longer-term goals, and so on. Once you know how to LEAP, you will be able to unlock the impasse and persuade the other person to help you get what you really need. And, most important, you will do that without falling victim to the debilitating anger and frustration that too often end up wreaking havoc with your relationship.

The truth is that, even though your adversary may not be a close friend, a loved one, or a family member, your relationship with that person is important to you—at least in the moment. If it weren't, you wouldn't be arguing in the first place, because you'd be willing and able to walk away. On the face of it some arguments are about unimportant things, but in the moment you're arguing they don't feel that way because oftentimes the overt issues are a proxy for the real argument that lies beneath. The only time you can really be in a "who cares what you think?" situation with another person is if you don't care about the person, don't care if the person continues to care about you, or don't *need* anything from that person.

So, what I'm going to be telling you is as much about preserving relationships and creating partnerships as it is about getting what you need. In fact, one of the things I'm going to be explaining is why you *must* first preserve that relationship in order to get what you need. That is why LEAP is much more than a method for conflict resolution. It is a set of well-studied psychological principles and specific skills that will make you more effective and fulfilled in all your relationships.

LEAP is new, but it relies on what came before—from the many philosophical traditions I quoted above, from the science of psychology, and from common sense. It is a method for easily remembering and using age-old truths in your everyday life. Like a melody that is catchy and hard to forget, once you learn LEAP you will find that you can call it up any time you need it.

Your Part in This

I've been using this method in my own psychotherapy practice and teaching it to laypeople in seminars for many years. Its efficacy is not only scientifically based but also practically proven. It will work for you just as it has for thousands of others so long as you practice it with sincerity, honesty, and a true desire to move forward instead of staying stuck. The key word here is "practice." If you're anything like the people who come to my seminars, and I think you probably are, much of what you will learn in this book will ring true to you. And if you're anything like me, you will, nevertheless, sometimes keep taking the bait and diligently argue your way into another impasse, all the while thinking, "That made sense when I read it, but it doesn't work!"

In those instances it's the lack of practice that leads me astray. Practice is essential. So after you've read a chapter, try out what you learned the next chance you get. Read this book with a highlighter and reread the sections you highlighted. Or, if using a highlighter is not your style, dog-ear those pages you want to be sure to remember. Mark my words, as you read, lightbulbs are going to go off. Make sure you note the pages where that happened so you can easily go back to them.

When you're done with the book, go back and read only the dog-eared pages. And take five minutes to go back and read the boxed quotes and lists you will see in the pages ahead.

It's just like learning a song for the first time. You don't learn the entire song the very first time you hear it. You have to repeat it until you get all the words and the melody memorized. But once it's in your head, it's impossible to forget.

SO WHATEVER HAPPENED to my statistics test? I went home after that frustrating conversation, calmed myself down, and considered my options. The next morning, I called the professor again, only this time I focused on understanding and appreciating his point of view rather than on persuading him with my arguments. I wanted to lower his defenses and look for what *he* needed in order to give me what I needed.

"I'm sorry to call again," I said when he picked up the phone. "I just wanted to get a better understanding of your position. Would you mind if I asked you a couple of questions?"

"My position is the same," he said defensively. "I'm not going to go back and forth on this."

"I understand, and I promise I won't argue with you. I'm sorry if I was a bit overbearing yesterday."

"As I said, I'm sorry about your situation," he said, softening and giving his own apology in response to mine. "I can see why you felt you had to make the case. What is it you want to know?"

"You mentioned that letting me take the test again would set a bad precedent. Is that right?" I asked, reflecting back what I'd heard him say the previous day.

"That's correct. I've never done it, and if I do it for you there will be no end to it."

"That would be extremely annoying," I said empathizing with his feelings. "I teach several undergraduate courses, and I know I would be annoyed if every student who failed a test asked to take it again."

"Yes, it would," he agreed.

"I'm curious. How many people over the years have asked you what I asked?"

After what felt like an eternity of silence he said, "Actually, I can't think of anyone who's asked me to do that in the twenty years I've been teaching the course."

"Well, maybe that's because you have this rule and most people know not to ask." I wanted to say that if no one had asked in twenty years it was obviously not going to be a problem for him to let me re-take the test. But I held my tongue and kept my focus on understanding him rather than contesting him.

"Perhaps," he said.

"Can I ask one last question?"

"Go ahead."

"If by chance you had done this in the past and just aren't remembering it now, would that make a difference?"

"Well, if there were a precedent I would have to reconsider."

I thanked him and rushed to call David, who had been Professor Cohen's teaching assistant for several years. David told me that five years before someone in the professor's class had failed and taken the final over. That was the reason he'd originally suggested I call and ask for a second chance. David called Professor Cohen to remind him of this fact, and I retook the test the following morning. I passed with a B, graduated on schedule, and started my new job.

If I had not called the professor back with my new focus—lowering his defenses and listening with the goal of understanding what it was he needed rather than arguing the merits of my case—the impasse we reached in that first conversation would have been the last word.

PART ONE

Getting Ready to LEAP

1

I'm Right, You're Wrong—
How to Recognize
When You've Reached an Impasse

Doubt is not a pleasant condition, but certainty is absurd.

—Voltaire

I have a neighbor who has a lot of opinions, most of them negative, about goings-on in the neighborhood. The single-lane country road we live on is nearly deserted, so I often walk my dog, Carli, off the leash. A cousin who was visiting me took Carli for a walk and was confronted by this neighbor—we'll call her Mrs. Kravitz—who shouted, "That dog should be on a leash!" and then admonished her grandchild to "stay away from that dog, she bites!" When my cousin relayed this false accusation, I was livid. Carli had never done anything of the kind, and I thought about knocking on Mrs. Kravitz's door and giving her a piece of my mind.

At this point, I should explain how I feel about Carli. She was a stray wandering the streets of New York City when she adopted me. Over the years she's licked my tears when loved ones died, dogged my every footstep when I am at home, wrestled gently with the children in my life, and made me laugh every time I see the insane passion she has for chasing her ball. Until I met Carli I never understood how people could love their dogs almost like children. I get it now.

When I told my cousin I intended to confront my neighbor, however, he didn't seem to think it was such a good idea. "What's the point?" he asked. I thought for a moment and realized the only purpose would be to strike back, to tell Mrs. Kravitz she was dead wrong! In fact, nothing would be gained except a momentary venting of my anger. I didn't need to change my neighbor's mind and I didn't need her permission to walk my dog off the leash. If I had talked to her with no other goal than to vent my anger, I would have been throwing gasoline on the fire. I would have said something like, "How dare you lie about Carli! You've known her for seven years and you can't name a single instance when she bit someone. What the hell is wrong with you?" Instead, I ignored the accusation, gave my neighbor a wide berth, and the dust settled. I know I'm right and she's wrong, and I am able to leave it at that. I also know that disagreements do not always have to become arguments, and not all arguments end at an impasse. Some disagreements are of the "let sleeping dogs lie" variety. There's an impasse, but nothing will be gained by trying to break it.

Healthy Arguments

Unlike my disagreement with Mrs. Kravitz, however, many disagreements do require a resolution because something needs to be done, something has been asked for, or some decision must be made. We can't ignore them. For the most part, assuming the argument is healthy (that is, the opponents have some trust, they listen to and treat each other with respect), such disagreements rarely end at an impasse. And if they do, the dead end is typically short-lived and poses no harm to the relationship. Let's look at an example.

I once had a disagreement with a colleague, a fellow professor at Columbia University, about whether one of our mutual doctoral students, who was analyzing data for her dissertation, should be allowed to consult with a statistician. I will call this colleague Professor David Holt. Professor Holt is an expert in statistics and I am anything but. In fact, more than twenty years ago, when I was accepted to graduate school, I was told by the chair of New York University's Ph.D. program in clinical psychology that I had achieved the distinction of having by far the worst math scores of anyone ever admitted to the program during its entire thirty-year history! I take some consolation in believing that he was, in fact, giving me a backhanded compliment, saying that my other talents outweighed this obvious limitation. But the simple truth was, and still is, that I have a tough time with math.

During a meeting with our student Mary, she asked us if she could hire a statistician to help her with a particularly complex set of analyses. Since I often use such consultants myself, I immediately said yes and asked her whom she had in mind. She began to answer when Professor Holt weighed in.

"Hold on, Mary," he said. "I didn't say I approved of your hiring someone for this."

"Is there a problem?" I asked.

"Yes. It's not appropriate for a student to hire someone to complete part of her thesis. It's not ethical. You shouldn't suggest that it is."

Mary flashed a worried glance my way, surely thinking I had been offended by the accusation that I had just told her to do something unethical. But I had known David a long time and was not offended or feeling defensive because we trusted each other. Still, I took the bait in the playful spirit of an academic debate.

"You think that if she has a statistician conduct the analyses and write up the results for her, it would be a form of plagiarism?" I asked, reflecting back what I had heard.

"Essentially, yes."

"I guess I would have to agree with you then," I said.

Smiling mischievously now, because he knew I was laying a trap for him, David said, "Then we're agreed. Mary won't use a consultant."

Mary looked crestfallen, so I quickly jumped in. "He's joking. We're not done talking about this yet. *Professor Holt*," I continued, using his academic title to signal the start of a more serious debate, "are there any circumstances you can imagine when it would be appropriate for an investigator to hire a statistical consultant to do research?"

Smiling, he said, "You hired me on your last grant from the NIH. I don't see anything unethical about that because I was credited as coauthor on the paper we published from that research."

"And how is this different?"

"Mary will be the only author of her thesis. The statistician you propose she hire will not have authorship, yet he or she will have written some of the thesis in addition to performing the analyses. That's the difference."

"Maybe we should just drop the whole idea," Mary interjected, nervous about where she thought this was headed.

"Bear with us," I reassured her, and then turned back to David. "Didn't you help Mary with her last round of analyses?"

"Yes, I did."

"Who was sitting at the computer keyboard? Who was designating the variables and actually running the analyses?"

"I was. I see where you're going, Xavier, but that was different."

"Why?"

"Because every step of the way I was teaching Mary, explaining what we had to do and why, and then—most important, I should add—asking her to explain it back to me so I knew she understood."

"And that's exactly how we should handle the work she does with the statistician. If she cannot tell us, in her own words, what was done and why, then I agree we have a problem."

"What about the actual writing?" David asked, appearing to give some ground.

"The tables from those analyses—didn't you give them to her?"

"I gave her the raw output, but she put the tables together, and I certainly didn't write her results section."

"And that's exactly how we should handle her work with the consultant, don't you think?"

"I see your point," David conceded. Then, smiling at Mary, he said, "Well, you can't hire me, that would be a conflict, but maybe I can save you some money and we can look at these analyses together."

That's how Mary got the help she needed—for free. I got the satisfaction of convincing my colleague to agree to my proposal, and Professor Holt got to keep a consultant out of the mix. Why did our initial disagreement turn into a friendly argument that ended well for all parties involved? Because it was healthy. We went into it with a great deal of respect for and trust in one another. But not just any kind of trust; we showed a very specific kind of trust that is crucial for engaging in a productive argument that ends well. We both trusted that, first and foremost, we would be listened to. Second, we trusted that we would not be personally attacked, called names, or disparaged in other ways. Third, and most important, we each trusted that we were well liked, if not loved, by the other person. David and I liked one another a great deal and had even developed a kind of love. This last form of trust may be hard for you to accept at the moment, and your defenses may be going up a bit—*Here comes the touchy-feely psychobabble BS!*—but by the end of this book you will have a much clearer idea of what I mean by love in this context and why I think it is the guiding star for any argument. When you feel respected, trusted, liked, and even loved, you will be at your best: open, curious, flexible, and willing to give. And when you give those things with sincerity, you get the same in return. Under these conditions no impasse is impenetrable.

> When you feel respected, trusted, liked, and even loved, you will be at your best: open, curious, flexible, and willing to give. And when you give those things with sincerity, you get the same in return. Under these conditions no impasse is impenetrable.

I argue every day. So do you. Gerry Spence, the famous trial lawyer, writes in his best-selling book *How to Argue and Win Every Time*, that "Everyone wants to argue. Everyone does. Everyone needs to . . . We must argue—to help, to warn, to love, to create, to learn, to enjoy justice—to be." And I agree, as I do with much of his advice. Mr. Spence shows his readers how to win healthy arguments like the one I describe above. Indeed, in a courtroom—and I have been in many because of my work as a forensic expert—there are rules in place to ensure that the arguing parties listen to one another (only one person may talk at a time and every single word is recorded), are treated with respect, and do not engage in name-calling. These arguments still turn toxic, but far less easily and commonly than they do outside the courtroom in everyday life. And when one does, the judge will usually stop the argument and call the offending parties to the bench to admonish them.

Under normal circumstances, however, you don't have a judge to help you change course when your argument goes south. And you don't need one, because with LEAP you'll have the tools you need to infuse health into an argument that has become toxic, created an impasse, and damaged your relationship. But before you can use those tools, you need to know how to recognize those instances when they are needed. The earlier you use them, the more quickly the impasse will be broken and the less damage you will do to your relationship.

Toxic Arguments: From Partners to Enemies in Six Seconds

Ray and Bob were good friends who occasionally worked together. An entrepreneur, Ray had hired Bob to design a software package, which he then sold to a client. One warm summer afternoon they were standing by the barbecue, each having drunk almost a six-pack of beer. The occasion was intended as a celebration of the sale, but when Ray announced what Bob's share of the sale price would be, the atmosphere turned decidedly tense. Bob looked anything but happy, and, seeing that his friend was ten miles from pleased with the news, Ray asked if there was a problem. Bob, uncomfortable because he appreciated the work, nevertheless said that there was. "To be honest, that's not what I was expecting."

"Well, I'm glad you're finally being honest," Ray said. "What exactly were you expecting?"

A little put off by his friend's sarcasm, Bob went straight to the heart of the matter. "You told me when we started that I would be getting ten percent of the sale, and now you're telling me I am getting half that."

"I never said that!" Ray practically shouted, beer spraying from his mouth.

"You absolutely did. Come on. Do you really think I would have dropped everything for two weeks to work on this if you hadn't promised a bonus?"

"Are you saying I'm lying?"

"No. Maybe you just don't remember."

"I told you I wanted to put this in writing, but you said I didn't have to. Now maybe I know why."

"I didn't forget anything. Ten percent is ten percent!"

"I *said* you would get ten percent of *my* profit, not of the *sale* price," Ray stated slowly, as if he were speaking to a child.

"That's not what you said, Ray."

"So you *are* saying I'm lying!"

LET'S STOP HERE and have a look at what's happening. The health of this argument is failing fast. The concrete is already starting to dry on the impasse. Bob and Ray have gone round and round—I count four times—each essentially accusing the other of being dead wrong while maintaining his own complete infallibility. No ifs, ands, or buts about it. They should have stopped at the very first dead end, at the first "I'm right, you're wrong":

> BOB: "You told me when we started that I would be getting ten percent of the sale, and now you're telling me I am getting half that."
>
> RAY: "I never said that!"
>
> BOB: "You absolutely did . . ."

Instead, with every go-round the argument intensified and both friends, feeling insulted, flung insults in response. Ray felt he was being called a liar. Bob should have stopped the moment he heard that; instead, he took the bait and said, "Maybe you just forgot." Now, that may sound like he's giving his friend the benefit of the doubt, and he is in a way. But it is also another way of saying "I'm right" while adding a more subtle insult. Because the unspoken but implied accusation is that Ray unconsciously manipulated the situation. He *conveniently forgot* what he had promised. This is a form of name-calling—*you unconsciously wanted to screw me*—that is hard to detect at first because it is so subtle. At best it was not a compliment, and it had the effect of throwing fuel on the fire.

Look at the result. What was Ray's reaction to Bob's statement that he probably just forgot? An insult to match the one he felt he'd been given: "I told you I wanted to put this in writing, but you said I didn't have to. Now maybe I know why." Whether his friend meant it that way, Ray heard "you forgot" as an accusation that he had changed the deal on purpose, albeit unconsciously. So he flung the same insult back, but more bluntly. By doing that, he opened up a whole new battlefront. Ray had wanted to write down the terms of their agreement, which would have eliminated the problem. One can easily imagine him thinking, "But nooo, you didn't want to do that. Maybe now I know why!" Bob's suggestion that Ray may have forgotten was not a bad idea, but delivered when it was and in the way it was, it led to a toxic argument.

The Seven Habits of Healthy Fighting

When you win an argument, you can either feel closer to and more trusting of the person you were arguing with or you can feel more distrustful and distant. I tell couples all the time that if their fights are healthy, it should be bringing them closer together. And if it's a business or some other kind of relationship, a healthy argument should leave the opponents feeling respected and positive about each other. There are seven habits of healthy fighting that can get you there. Like exercise and low-fat diets for heart disease, these habits will not only help to keep you healthy, but will help you to avoid toxic arguments.

The Seven Habits of Healthy Fighting
1. Stop insisting you're right.
2. Don't engage in insults or name-calling.
3. Pick the right time.

4. Never use absolutes.
5. Don't "kitchen-sink it."
6. Listen without defending.
7. Reflect back what you have heard.

To illustrate the importance of these seven habits, let's look at an even more toxic argument. I met Kimberly and Jason while I was working on a documentary for ABC News about how arguments can push a marriage to the brink of divorce. With automatic video cameras installed in Kimberly and Jason's home, ABC taped more than fifty hours of their arguments over a period of months. Kimberly is the host of an early-morning radio program in upstate New York and Jason is the stay-at-home father of their eight-year-old daughter, Chloe. The family had moved to the area because of Kimberly's career, and Jason had grown resentful of the fact that he'd given up his own career to care for Chloe. Here is an excerpt from an argument that started when Jason said he didn't think Kimberly appreciated all he was doing for her and the family:

JASON: I'm a friggin' stay-at-home dad that makes nothing, and I put up with everything, humiliation, everything.

KIMBERLY: You know what? You could have gone to work a year ago.

JASON: A year ago? Really! Where?

KIMBERLY: Wherever you wanted to go to work.

JASON: Where? Tell me.

KIMBERLY: I don't know!

JASON: Oh, come on, Miss Answers, tell me the answer!

KIMBERLY: I'm not responsible for you. Why am I responsible for you?

JASON: You had the question, and obviously you had the answer, because you brought it up.

KIMBERLY: You sit around whining.

JASON: [voices overlap] What am I getting? What am I getting?

KIMBERLY: And wondering why no one gives you anything.

JASON: [voices overlap] I, I'm nothing but a freaking slave to everybody.

KIMBERLY: Okay. Okay. I'm guessing we're going to have the conversation in front of Chloe.

JASON: Well, what am I getting?

KIMBERLY: Well, why does anybody owe you anything, Jason?

JASON: [voices overlap] You obviously have the answer.

KIMBERLY: No, nobody owes you anything.

JASON: I never said peop—anybody owes me anything.

KIMBERLY: Well, then, quit feeling sorry for yourself. Poor me!

JASON: All right. Well, kiss my butt!

At this point on the videotape you can see Chloe sighing heavily. What, if anything, was being gained by this exchange? One might argue that both Jason and Kimberly were blowing off steam. But, in fact, they later stated that they felt angrier after the exchange than they had when they started it. Let's look at the healthy habits that were missing.

1. Stop insisting you're right.

Kimberly and Jason just went round and round, repeating their positions and solidifying the impasse they were building. Jason's position was that his wife did not appreciate him and especially the fact that he had given up his job to support hers; Kimberly's position was that he was exaggerating and whining—he was wrong and could work if he wanted. What was achieved by going round and round? Nothing.

> Whenever you insist you're right, you accomplish absolutely nothing other than raising the other person's defenses and stubbornness about their own point of view.

If you find yourself repeating your position more than once, without being asked, you're insisting that you're right. If you raise your voice whenever you express your view, it's the same effect. And whenever you insist you're right, you accomplish absolutely nothing other than raising the other person's defenses and stubbornness about their own point of view.

2. Don't engage in insults or name-calling.

Although Kimberly's accusation "You sit around whining" is not technically name-calling—she didn't say, "You're a whiner"—I know Jason heard it that way. He later revealed that he also heard "quit feeling sorry for yourself. Poor me!" as another insult. He felt Kimberly was calling him a martyr. When he called her "Miss Answers," Jason was being more direct than Kimberly. And predictably she felt he was accusing her of being arrogant and impossible.

> Whenever we engage in name-calling we make people defensive, angrier, and more rigid.

Whether you think either of them was correct in their assessment is not the point. The point is that whenever we engage in name-calling we make people defensive, angrier, and more rigid.

Sometimes name-calling is obvious. When you hear yourself calling someone an idiot, stupid, selfish, irrational, and so on, you can expect him to become defensive and to get sidetracked from solving the problem as you fling insults back and forth. Other times, name-calling is more subtle. If you hear yourself labeling your opponent's point of view as naïve, stupid, or irrational, I guarantee that he will hear it as your calling *him* naïve, stupid, or irrational. And then there are the hot buttons we all have, the coded insults that make us go ballistic. Like when my friend's husband argues with her about money, he sometimes says, "You're just like your mother." This is not necessarily an insult . . . unless you knew her mother!

3. Pick the right time.

Their timing was terrible in that they argued while clearly overcome by anger. Even without seeing the tape you probably understood just how angry they were by some of the things they said ("friggin'," "kiss my butt"), the fact that they kept interrupting and talking over one another, that they were calling each other names, and by the poor judgment they showed in continuing to argue in front of their daughter, even after they recognized they were doing so.

On a more positive note, they did not involve their daughter by trying to make her choose sides. Nevertheless, when they were later asked to reflect on the wisdom of arguing in front of Chloe, they both agreed it could not have been good for her and that her presence also made them both feel more defensive.

Don't address a potentially explosive issue when you're heading out the door to work, or at the end of a very long day, or when your adversary is obviously irritable. There may be no ideal time, but you must recognize that some times are better than others, and some times are just plain bad.

4. *Never use absolutes.*

Kimberly and Jason were both experts at using absolutes. "You *always* nag, nag, nag," Jason said repeatedly during their fights. "You *never* think about me; it's *always* about you," was one of Kimberly's mantras. The response to such absolutes is always more defensiveness.

During another part of their argument, when Kimberly said, "It's *always* something, you're *never satisfied* . . . ," Jason launched right into a defensive mode. And no wonder. It's unlikely he heard anything other than those two little words "always" and "never." He would have heard them as criticisms, which indeed they are. Unfortunately, he was too angry and defensive to hear anything *but* those two words. The result was an impasse.

> Using absolutes is like hitting the mute button on your vocal cords. Your lips are still moving but no sound can be heard.

To be fair, I was present for another situation in which the couple were fighting over Jason's desire to have more than one "boys' night out" that week. As Jason repeated Kimberly's words, "always" and "never" came up like an ugly chorus. Kimberly tensed up, and a shadow came over her face, as soon as Jason accused her of *always* being unhappy with him and *always* trying to control him. And what was her response? Her blood began to boil and she tuned out.

When we speak in absolutes, when we accuse someone of never doing such and such or of unequivocally being wrong, we are usually not telling the truth (no one is any one way 100 percent of the time) and asking for a defensive volley in return. What's more, we are practically ensuring that the other person will stop listening to our position. Using absolutes is like hitting the mute button on your vocal cords. Your lips are still moving but no sound can be heard.

By all accounts Benjamin Franklin was a master at diplomacy, which is, by the way, the art of breaking an impasse in order to find mutually satisfying resolutions. In his autobiography, Franklin writes, "I made it a rule to forbear all direct contradiction to the sentiment of others, and all positive assertion of my own. I even forbade myself the use of every word or expression in the language that imported a fix'd opinion, such as 'certainly,' 'undoubtedly,' etc. . . . And this mode, which I at first put on with some violence to my natural inclination, became at length so easy, and so habitual to me, that perhaps for these fifty years past no one has ever heard a dogmatical expression escape me." In short, as Franklin clearly understood, being 100 percent certain about anything and using absolutes gives the person you are arguing with no room to maneuver—which equates to having no way to save face—and no option but to return fire.

If you find yourself accusing someone of always or never doing something, you are using absolutes. And if, unlike Ben Franklin, you feel compelled to convey your 100 percent confidence in your opinion with words like "undoubtedly," "certainly," and "obviously," you can expect your adversary to become defensive and more entrenched in his opinion.

5. Don't "kitchen-sink it."

Kimberly and Jason were also adept at kitchen-sinking it: their fights never stayed focused on one topic. Instead, more and more hurts and loosely related accusations were heaped onto the smoldering ruins of the initial disagreement. For example, Jason felt he should be allowed to go out to a neighborhood bar at the end of the day after Kimberly returned home from work and the family had dinner together. He liked going out as many as five nights a week and believed it was his right to socialize after being home all day doing housework. He invited Kimberly to go along, but because she had to get up early for work she was usually going to bed by the time he was ready to go out. Kimberly resented his going to the bar, and she was also worried that he might be cheating on her. This was a major impasse with serious underlying issues. Jason felt he should be able to go out as often as he wanted after his wife went to bed, and Kimberly felt he shouldn't go out more than once a week. Neither of them was willing to give an inch. Each time the subject came up, Jason reiterated the fact that to support Kimberly's career move he had left a job he loved. Because of this, and the many other sacrifices he liked to enumerate, he felt it was his "right" to go out. As he rumbled on about the list of concessions he had made for the sake of his wife and family, the original issue was soon obscured by the volcanic ash of several years' worth of complaints. Kimberly, for her part, tried to defend against every new accusation. Thus, instead of fighting a single battle, they ended up fighting a war on several fronts simultaneously, often forgetting what the original disagreement had been about.

If you find that you cannot remember how an argument started, you are involved in kitchen-sinking it and are bound to get nowhere but further from a solution.

> If you find that you cannot remember how an argument started, you are involved in kitchen-sinking it and are bound to get nowhere but further from a solution.

---

6. Listen without defending.

Looking back at the excerpts above, I cannot find one instance in which either spouse clearly heard what the other had to say without feeling compelled to defend him- or herself and go on the counterattack. Did Jason even hear a word his wife was saying? She was telling him she also felt unappreciated, and his response was to accuse her of criticizing him. He didn't really listen to what she said; he reacted to it—defensively. And because Kimberly did not feel listened to, she spoke louder and more adamantly, while at the same time trying to defend herself against the new accusation. But Kimberly was no better at listening without being defensive and attacking than Jason was. When she defended herself against his complaint by accusing him of being the cause of his own misery, nothing was gained. And their trust, respect for one another, and ability to control their anger were eroded even further.

If you find yourself saying "but," you are likely defending rather than listening, as in "I hear what you said, but I . . ." If you notice that your adversary is getting defensive, chances are you are, too.

7. Reflect back what you have heard.

Reflecting back what someone has said to you is a powerful tool. In fact, it is the cornerstone of the LEAP method. It involves letting the other person know you have heard what he said and that you understand his perspective. It is as effective at lowering the temperature of an argument and building trust as it is simple. But this tool is often overlooked. Kimberly and Jason are no exception. If you look back at their exchange you will not see one instance in which either of them reflected back what the other said. Each expression of hurt, each opinion or complaint, appears to be ignored. The speaker never has the experience of knowing that the listener has actually heard and understood him. Let me show you what I mean.

> JASON: I'm a friggin' stay-at-home dad that makes nothing, and I put up with everything, humiliation, everything.
>
> KIMBERLY: You know what? You could have gone to work a year ago.

Do you think Jason felt he was understood? Sure, his words were heard, because Kimberly's defense and counterattack were clearly based on them. But was he understood? Had she reflected back what she heard, she might have said something like, "If I heard you right, you feel humiliated because you're a stay-at-home dad. Is that right?" I don't have to wonder what Jason's reaction would have been to her saying those words, because soon after this exchange I taught Kimberly how to reflect back what she heard, and the result was one I've seen countless times. Jason became less angry, felt closer to Kimberly, and was better able to listen to her. Because he felt she understood his perspective—not that she agreed with it—he was able to lower his defenses.

If the person you're arguing with accuses you of not listening or not understanding them, they're right. This is one of those instances when the judge and jury reside solely in the person who feels misunderstood or not heard. If someone says, "You just don't get it," chances are you have not been reflecting back what you heard.

> If the person you're arguing with accuses you of not listening or not understanding them, they're right.

THESE SEVEN HEALTHY habits apply to every kind of argument and are so important that I will list them here again.

1. Stop insisting you're right—there's nothing to be gained by becoming adamant and it always makes your opponent more stubborn.
2. Don't engage in insults or name-calling—it will only make people defensive, angrier, and rigid.
3. Pick the right time—pay attention to whether your adversary is too angry, defensive, tired, or stressed to be receptive to you.
4. Never use absolutes—people get defensive and more entrenched when absolutes are used against them.
5. Don't "kitchen-sink it"—bringing in past transgressions escalates anger and defensiveness, and derails you from the issue at hand.
6. Listen without defending—when you are defensive the person will not feel heard or understood and will be more defensive themselves.
7. Reflect back what you have heard—this is one of the most effective ways you can lower the temperature of an argument and at the same time open someone up to your point of view.

Toxic Arguments:
The Three Es to Watch Out For

Now that you have a picture of these healthy habits, how do you recognize when they've gone missing? There are three common warning signs that an argument has become toxic and is certain to damage your relationship. I call them the three Es: evasion, escalation, and entropy.

- **Evasion:** One or both of you avoids discussion of the subject altogether because you never get anywhere and you're totally frustrated.
- **Escalation:** Whenever you do talk about it, things just get worse—accusations fly, you're calling one another names—and you end up feeling angrier or more depressed than when you started. Kimberly and Jason were, unfortunately, highly adept at escalation.
- **Entropy:** The toxic argument has robbed you both of the energy you need to resolve the disagreement. Nothing is getting done and no one has the energy to revisit the problem.

The behaviors may sound rather childish to you, but as grown-ups we act a lot like children more often than we like to think. When a wife "forgets" to pick up her husband's suit at the cleaner because he "forgot" to pick up the milk, or when we get into an argument with a friend and then engage in a game of chicken to see who's going to make the first phone call, we are displaying one or more of the three Es.

People get into these power struggles all the time, and, like a wound that's become infected, they just fester until they've poisoned the relationship. That's why it's so important to recognize when an argument has turned toxic, so you can administer the antidote before the poison spreads. Here is an example from my personal life where all three Es can easily be seen.

I have four brothers. One is a recovering alcoholic, whom I will call

Sam. Today I am very proud of Sam. He is sober and open about the fact that he has a drinking problem. But that was not always the case. Some years ago my mother phoned me to say that Sam was coming to live with her rent-free because he was "between jobs." I was immediately critical.

"Mom," I said, "he's not just between jobs! He's drinking again and I think this is a very bad idea."

"Ay, Dios mio!" she said, slipping back into Spanish, as she always did when upset. "He's your brother, you shouldn't say such things!"

"But it's the truth. He called me just last night and he was slurring his words. You must know he's drinking again."

"He told me he's not drinking. You shouldn't say that. That's not being a good brother. Family needs to stick together."

"I am too a good brother. Look, he's told you he's not drinking before and then you've found him passed out—come on, you're in denial!" No answer. Then her sobs could be heard. I said, "I know you don't like hearing this, but in a week or two you're going to call and ask me to talk to him again because he's drinking. You're going to tell me you can't live with him when he's like this and ask me to tell him to move out. You're not helping him by denying the problem."

"Enough!" she shouted into the phone. "Your brother said he was not drinking and I believe him. Enough." I could hear her sobbing again, so I ended the conversation by saying, "Fine, have it your way, but don't call me to ask for help when you find him drunk and passed out."

We had reached an impasse. I was sure I was right and she was sure I was wrong. We both were angry. Although her anger subsided when I later apologized for saying she couldn't call me and assured her that she could, my apology didn't resolve the impasse.

In the weeks that followed we both tried evasion. We talked about anything but how it was going with Sam. Then she called me one day and more or less confessed that he "might" be drinking, but she didn't think so. Still stuck on wanting to be right—instead of focusing on what I needed, which was for her to set some limits with my brother—I once again confronted her denial. Predictably the phone call turned into an argument during which we both, once again, escalated by calling one another names (she's a denier and I'm a bad brother), not listening, and certainly not reflecting back an understanding of the other's position. She was, after all, Sam's mother, and it was much harder for her to see and accept what was happening than it was for me. My mother was fiercely protective of her children. No bad word could be spoken about any of her angels—myself included. But at the time I didn't use that insight to calm myself down enough to practice any of the healthy arguing habits—even though I knew what they were.

Very quickly, after just a few rounds, entropy took over. We avoided the topic altogether. It wasn't until Sam had a full-blown relapse and ended up with a DUI that we talked about it again. Unfortunately, by that time the argument was moot—I took no pleasure in being right, and although I was later able to repair it, some damage had been done to my relationship with my mother.

Practice the seven habits of healthy fighting and learn to recognize the three Es. By doing that you will begin to turn the tide and set the stage for getting what you need. Now, don't think you have to get it right all at once. Or even that you could. Chances are you've been approaching arguments in your own way for a very long time. Recognize that, and know that attempting to master a new skill all at once is a surefire way to ensure that you reach a very big impasse with yourself! So think back on some of the fights you've had with friends and loved ones—the big ones, and the not-so-big ones. What are your patterns? Do you tend to engage in absolutes, thereby alienating the other person? Do you try to discuss the big-ticket emotional items at the very worst time, ensuring nothing but anger and ill will? Maybe you state your own case and then, instead of listening to your partner, wait until it's your turn to talk again? Or maybe you just try to evade the issue, hoping everything will return to the status quo, even though you know deep in your heart that will never happen. Whatever your habits, and whatever your style, know that by being aware of these warning signs and developing skills for healthy fighting you will be well on your way to getting what you need and strengthening your relationships in the process.

The tools I'll provide in the pages ahead will help you to do that, and so much more.

2

What Is It You Really Need?

You can't always get what you want.
But if you try sometime,
You just might find,
You get what you need.

—Mick Jagger and Keith Richards,
"You Can't Always Get What You Want"

The thing about an impasse is that it locks us into focusing on the wrong goal. Over and over again I see people lose sight of the forest for the trees. The big picture—what they really need—gets lost as they focus on those magic words they think they need to hear: "I admit it, I was wrong and you were right."

That's not what you need.

That's just what you want in that moment.

There is a big difference between the two.

During my many arguments with my brother Henry about whether he had a mental illness, I was repeatedly seduced into an impasse. It seemed that all I wanted was for him to say, "I am sick and I need help" (that is, to tell me I was right and he was wrong). I wanted him to wave the white flag. That single-minded quest was fruitless because we had this argument over and over again with the same result. The problem was that I'd lost sight of what I really needed—for him to agree to take his medicine. Once I was able to focus on that, I stopped pushing, and, as a result, he had no reason to continue pushing back. From that point on, we were no longer at an impasse, and I began to make progress very quickly. For more than ten years now he has taken his medicine, even though he's still not sure he has an illness. He's never waved the white flag, and I don't need him to.

The Problem with Being Right

Stephen, a restaurateur who uses LEAP to train his waitstaff to avoid impasses and stay focused on the bigger picture—making the customers happy so everyone makes money—provided another, perhaps more common example of how quickly a disagreement can come to an impasse when we lose sight of the big picture, and how counterproductive that can be. One night Lisa, one of his waitresses, came to him in the middle of a busy dinner service, rolled her eyes, and said, "Table six wants to talk to the manager." According to Stephen, their conversation went something like this:

"What's the problem?"

"The mother claims I brought her son the wrong order, but I didn't. I brought him the cheeseburger he asked for."

"What did you say to them?"

"Exactly what I just told you. That I brought what the kid ordered."

"Why do they want to talk to me?"

"I don't know." She shrugged. "I took back the burger and brought them what they said they wanted."

When Stephen spoke with the mother, he learned that although Lisa had brought out a different meal as requested, the customer was angry because of the way she did it. She said, "I know what my son ordered and he never ordered that cheeseburger. That girl was rude. You should train your staff that the customer is always right!"

"I am so sorry. What did Lisa say to you?"

"She said I was wrong, but that *she* would take care of it *anyway*."

Stephen was pleased that Lisa had changed the order and didn't charge her customer, but he was unhappy that she had made the woman angry. In a way, Lisa got what she deserved when she told the woman she was wrong but she, Lisa, would take care of it anyway—a knee-jerk defensive reaction. Now the woman wanted to *take care of*

Lisa by complaining to her boss. Later that night, when Stephen spoke to Lisa about the incident, he asked her why she had stuck to her guns about being right.

"Because I was. I wrote it down. I know what her son ordered. But I did what you told us to do—assume that the customer is always right—so I took it back to the kitchen and ordered a different meal for him."

"Ahh, but you're telling me the customer was wrong, and you made a point of telling her, too."

"Well, she was."

"What kind of tip did you get?"

"Nothing. She stiffed me!"

"Want to know what I think?" Stephen asked.

"Of course."

"I don't care who was right. You might have been right or she might have been right. It doesn't matter to me."

"Oh, so it doesn't matter to you whether I write the order down correctly?" Lisa asked sarcastically.

"Of course it does. You know that as well as I do. But no one's perfect. We all make mistakes from time to time. In the end, though, I don't care who made the mistake. What I want is for customers to go home happy, leave you a big tip, come again, and tell their friends to eat here. I also want them to treat you with respect. Was she disrespectful?"

"She called me incompetent!"

"Did she really?"

"Not literally, but it felt that way."

"Did you convince her that you were right?"

"No. Obviously not. She stiffed me on the tip."

In the heat of the moment Lisa lost sight of the big picture. Not only did she anger a customer and lose money as a result, but she also upset her boss, whom she liked a great deal. What Lisa should have done was to apologize for the mistake (even if she was sure she didn't make one) and bring out the new order. Really good servers are adept at apologizing without actually admitting it was their fault. When

Lisa's customer said, "I'm right, you're wrong," this is how it might have gone:

"This is not what we ordered."

"I am so sorry, what can I get you?"

> Many arguments are fueled by embarrassment and the threat of humiliation. In those instances people are defending their reputations or self-esteem rather than arguing a specific point. A well-placed apology will take the wind out of the sails of such arguments.

The "I am so sorry" could be an apology for making the mistake, it could be an implicit statement that the kitchen made the mistake, or it could be a simple expression of regret that *someone*—maybe even the customer!—made a mistake. The server, in this scenario, would not be saying, "I am so sorry that I made a mistake," but neither would she be blaming the customer and getting caught in an impasse as Lisa did.

Undoubtedly the customer would think the apology meant that the server agreed she'd made a mistake, and that's not necessarily a bad thing when you stop to think about it, because apologies allow people to save face. Many arguments are fueled by embarrassment and the threat of humiliation. In those instances people are defending their reputations or self-esteem rather than arguing a specific point. A well-placed apology will take the wind out of the sails of such arguments.

HERE IS ANOTHER example of how easy it is to lose sight of what you really need.

Angie was worried about her husband. James had gained more than one hundred pounds since they were first married, and both his parents had died from heart disease before the age of sixty-five. Based on conversations with her doctor and research she had done, Angie was certain that if James didn't lose weight he would suffer a similar fate.

She *wanted* him to admit he had a serious, life-threatening weight problem, but what she really *needed* was for him to lose the weight. Angie told me that whenever she tried to talk to James about his weight problem, they argued and ended up at an impasse. Their last argument had gone something like this:

"I'm very worried about your health and I feel that you're in denial about how serious a problem this is," Angie said, as she usually did whenever she brought up the issue. "If you don't do something about your weight, it's going to kill you!"

"You're overreacting and I am not in denial," James countered.

"But you are! Even Dr. Weber agrees with me."

"I haven't seen Dr. Weber in years. What does he know about me?"

"That's part of the problem—you need to make an appointment."

"No. The problem is you're overreacting again. Yeah, I'm a little heavy, but nothing like my mother and father. I check my blood pressure whenever I go to the pharmacy and it's fine."

"Checking your blood pressure with some machine is not the same as getting a checkup with your doctor!"

"I'm done arguing about this. I'm fine. You've got the problem. You're obsessed with dieting and you're overreacting."

"You're being a stubborn ass!"

You can probably see that several of the healthy habits of arguing were missing here. Angie and James were calling each other names (James is "in denial" and an "ass," and Angie is "overreacting"). Angie was kitchen-sinking (complaining that James has not gone to the doctor in years) when what she needed was to talk about his losing weight, and neither one of them was reflecting back what the other had said. Two of the three Es were evident as well (evasion—"I'm done arguing about this"—and escalation, as reflected in their kitchen-sinking).

I asked Angie, "If you could have only one thing, which of the following three would it be? James makes an appointment with his doctor? He admits his weight is a health problem? Or he becomes committed to losing weight?"

"Well, they're all connected. I can't choose just one of them," she answered.

"I appreciate that they're all connected. But think about it for a moment. Try to pick just one."

"Well, in that case, number three. I want him to lose the weight."

"Would you agree that's the thing you need the most?" I asked, to bring the point home.

"Yes, of course. That's the real issue."

"Then let's see how you can focus on that instead of the other two things you want."

"All right, how do we do that?"

"We start by finding out how James feels about the extra hundred pounds."

"But I already know that. It's not a problem for him."

"I don't know if you do know that. All you really know is that he doesn't have a weight problem as *you've* defined it. Do you honestly know how he feels about it in general? Is it creating other problems for him?"

"I guess I don't know that," she admitted.

Angie had argued herself into an impasse because James didn't see his weight as a health problem; he didn't see it her way. She'd already tried to *make* him see it her way and failed—many times over. It was time to take a new tack and find out if he had other reasons to want to lose weight.

> When you're in the heat of an argument you are going to become focused on what you think you want in the short term and end up with tunnel vision. This is a hardwired biological reflex and there's no sense fighting it. The trick is to not let it rule you.

Once I explained to Angie the seven habits of healthy fighting, she took a fresh stab at the problem. The next time they talked, she began the discussion very differently.

"I am sorry I keep pushing you about your weight and seeing the doctor. I realize I don't know how you feel about the extra weight you've gained. Can I talk to you about that if I promise not to argue about your health? I respect your opinion and won't try to convince you otherwise."

At first, James tried to evade the discussion by saying, "I don't have a health problem and don't want to talk about it." Obviously, he either hadn't heard or did not believe the reassurance she'd given him.

"I see your point. You don't have a health problem. I don't want to talk about that. Okay?" Angie said, reflecting back what she'd just heard instead of getting defensive.

"Well, what then?" James said, sounding somewhat less defensive.

"I'm just wondering how you feel about the weight in general. Is it slowing you down, do you feel it makes you less attractive?"

"So you're saying you're not attracted to me?" he asked, defenses rising again.

"No, no. I only know that when *I* gain weight I feel less attractive. I wonder if you've ever felt the same way."

In this conversation, Angie stayed focused on what she needed— rather than kitchen-sinking—and avoided calling James names. By doing that, she was able to lower her husband's defenses. By asking questions that indicated her genuine desire to understand how *he* felt about the weight and reflecting back his answers, she uncovered some reasons *James* had for wanting to lose weight, reasons that had nothing to do with confessing that she had been right all along. As it turned out, he admitted he was embarrassed by the extra hundred pounds he was carrying. He still didn't think his weight posed a health problem, but it did make him feel unattractive and it was slowing him down on the golf course.

Once Angie understood the problem as he defined it, they were able to talk about it again without getting into another impasse. Now that they had something they agreed on—less weight would make James feel more attractive and give him more energy—they were able to work together to help him take off the pounds. And because Angie was using LEAP, they were no longer having toxic arguments, which made them both feel happier and closer to one another. Eventually, James lost eighty pounds and a big weight was lifted off both their shoulders as they went from being adversaries to allies.

Tunnel Vision

When you're in the heat of an argument you are going to become focused on what you think you want in the short term and end up with tunnel vision. This is a hardwired biological reflex and there's no sense fighting it. To see how this works, let's talk for a moment about evolution and our nervous system. It's relevant.

Our nervous system is what it is because over hundreds of thousands of years of competition, it has survived. It has been designed and redesigned throughout centuries of human evolution, and the basic package we have today is a consequence of all that experience.

Among the functions that have developed in our nervous system is an alarm in our brain that helps us respond to threats. When the alarm goes off, our heart rate is elevated, the volume of blood flowing to our vital organs increases rapidly, and our attention becomes narrowly focused on the threat that's right in front of us. Think of a big spotlight versus a narrow laser beam—like the targeting laser on some rifles. When we are scared or angry, our attention goes from the spotlight— which illuminates a large area—to a pencil-thin beam that can light only one thing at a time. When we argue, we sense a threat and our alarm system is activated; we lose the wide beam and have only the narrowest pinpoint of light to focus our attention. It makes sense. If you were a primitive man or woman walking through a field of tall grass, gazing at the plains in front of you, the mountains in the distance, maybe even the clouds overhead, and then you heard a deep rumbling growl, all that larger landscape would disappear in a flash; you would focus only on the growl, seeing, hearing, and even smelling nothing else.

> When we are scared or angry, our attention goes from a spotlight—which illuminates a large area—to a pencil-thin beam that can light only one thing at a time.

What turns on this wonderfully effective alarm system is a particular part of your brain called the amygdala. Your brain has literally billions of nerve cells and many different lobes, or regions, that do very different things. What may come as a surprise to you, however, is that many parts of your brain are constantly in conflict with one another. There are countless examples of what neuropsychologists call *dual control systems* that are pushing and pulling against each other. For example, when you are reading this book you are using very fast eye movements—called saccadic eye movements—to move from one word to the next. But if you were to look up from the page and watch a car passing by, you would be using smooth pursuit eye movements. One type is very fast (saccadic) and you can consciously control it; the other (smooth pursuit) is very slow and you can control only when it starts and stops. You cannot consciously initiate a smooth pursuit eye movement unless there is something for you to track, such as a bird flying across the sky, but you can consciously make saccadic movements any time you like. These two types of eye movement share some brain regions, but they also have unique and separate circuitry. The separate circuits act like a seesaw. When one is powered up, it inhibits the other.

Similarly, the front part of your brain—simply called the frontal lobes—inhibits other parts of the brain. When damage to certain parts of the frontal lobes occurs, people's personalities often change. Rational, generally calm and sober people can become erratic, irritable, explosive, and highly emotional. The reason for this is that the frontal lobes have stopped inhibiting the part of their brain that makes them feel emotion.

The amygdala lies deeper in your brain, much closer to the brain stem and the rest of your body, than the frontal lobes. It is literally and figuratively closer to your heart. When you feel happy, sad, scared, or angry, more blood, glucose, and neurotransmitters (chemical messengers in the brain) are flowing into your amygdala to fuel the furnace of emotion. Whenever the furnace gets fired up, the frontal lobes—sooner or later—send messages to douse the flames. If they didn't, the first time you felt scared or angry could well be the last time. Without a governor (the frontal lobes), you would become so frightened and furious that you wouldn't be able to sleep or eat and would confront, perhaps even be violent toward, those who had angered you, or else you would run away and live like a hermit to escape the ever-increasing threats you perceived. Without frontal lobe inhibition you would not be able to stop and think. You could not assess whether the threats you perceived were real or imagined.

Brain Anatomy and Toxic Arguments

What does this brief lesson in brain anatomy and function have to do with toxic arguments? Everything. When we argue and feel attacked, we become defensive and angry. Our amygdala is literally fired up. Our feeling brain signals our sympathetic nervous system to dump adrenaline into our bloodstream; our heart pounds, our face flushes, we might sweat, and sometimes we even shake. Our thinking brain—the frontal lobes—processing the situation from higher ground, with a broader view, decides if we should continue the fight or step away from the conflict. Thus, when you say, "I don't know what came over me" or "I wasn't thinking," what you are really describing is your feeling brain overcoming your thinking brain and shutting it down temporarily.

That's one of the reasons people become violent and also why we often get stuck demanding that the person we are arguing with yield and admit he was wrong. Our more primitive, feeling brain—the science writer Carl Sagan called it our reptilian brain because, on an evolutionary scale, it is a lot like the brain of a reptile—is single-mindedly trying to push its way through the obstacle in front of it. Lacking frontal lobes, the reptilian brain cannot think to stop pushing, step back, and see the bigger picture, which would reveal how to get around the obstacle. When you're in the heat of an argument, it's as if

> When you say, "I don't know what came over me" or "I wasn't thinking," what you are really describing is your feeling brain overcoming your thinking brain and shutting it down temporarily.

you're hearing that growl. Your reptilian brain takes over, your frontal lobes shut down, and you will, even though it's ill advised, focus on what you want at the expense of what you really need.

You may be focused with laserlike clarity on wanting your prospective client to agree with *your* reasons for buying your product when what you really need is for him to sign on the dotted line. You may bullheadedly insist that your wife agree she's living beyond your means when you just need her to spend less. You could argue until you're blue in the face trying to get your teenager to agree that her plan to work as a waitress and surf after she graduates from high school is a bad idea, when you simply need her to agree to go to college.

Here is another example of how primitive instinct, your hardwired survival mechanism, may short-circuit the thinking process and stop you from getting what you need. You may recall that in 2007 Delta Air Lines emerged from bankruptcy. Major concessions from the pilots' union were a critical turning point for the faltering company. The pilots were focused on nothing but avoiding a deep salary cut. Escalation and evasion were readily apparent in news articles about the talks, which dragged on for several years as the two parties walked away from discussions again and again. Although management was reluctant to complain or engage in name-calling, the pilots' union was not. The union held demonstrations in the airline's biggest hub and complained bitterly to the press that the company was being unreasonable. The pilots were clearly angry, and the union was focusing on what they instinctively wanted—the management's agreement that it was wrong to request such deep pay cuts—instead of on what they actually needed, which was for the company to survive (because if it didn't, the pilots would not just be taking a pay cut; they'd all be out of a job). In effect, when their survival instinct took over, they could no longer see the bigger picture.

It was not until the very last minute that collapse was averted. Richard Bloch, the chairman of the arbitration panel that had been installed by court order as part of the Chapter 11 proceedings, ordered the union to return to the table and start negotiating immediately. He also gave a deadline, promising to void the pilots' current contract if they could not reach an agreement within the specified time. The pilots, on their part, promised to strike if that happened. Management said that if the pilots went on strike, Delta would have to shut down immediately. Now both sides had a vital shared interest—keeping the company up and running beyond the deadline. And with this shared crisis imminent, cooler heads finally prevailed.

Once both sides were able to see what they needed, which was to put aside their anger and work together to save the company, they were able to break the impasse. Their success was made clear in the press releases issued by both sides after they reached an agreement. The head of the pilots' union, speaking about the deep salary cuts they'd ultimately agreed to, said, "The new contract . . . provides real returns and job security for the unprecedented recent sacrifices made by the Delta pilots in support of our great company. We look forward to Delta's successful emergence from bankruptcy and together with all Delta employees, returning our airline to success." And the airline issued a statement praising the union, saying, "The additional pilot savings are a significant, necessary and appreciated component of Delta's restructuring plan." In the end, both management and the union focused on the big picture—saving the company—rather than on defeat or victory on the issue of the pay cuts. Neither of them said, "We were right and they were wrong." Less than a month later, Delta emerged from bankruptcy.

If you find yourself single-mindedly focusing on convincing the other person they are wrong, or insisting that there is only one solution to the impasse, your brain has probably put your amygdala in the driver's seat. Your nervous system is fired up and your ability to focus on the big picture is impaired. It's time to pull over and let your frontal lobes behind the wheel.

So how do you overcome hundreds of thousands of years of evolution and shut down your reptilian brain when you're in the heat of battle? In the case of the Delta pilots, an imminent crisis likely helped them to refocus on a new target, which was luckily the one that mattered. But how, other than being forced into it, can we change our focus to see what we really need? That will be the topic of chapter 5. But to use the tools I give you there, you will first need to prepare yourself mentally to let go of your prey (needing to be right). In order to let go you need to believe in the power of giving in order to receive. Let's talk about that.

3

Learning to Give in Order
to Get What You *Really* Need

You get the best out of others when you give the best of yourself.

—Harvey S. Firestone

For it is in giving that we receive.

—St. Francis of Assisi

During LEAP seminars, I ask attendees two questions: "Has being confrontational and sticking to your guns been working for you?" and "Has your relationship with the other person suffered as a result?" The answer to the first question is always "No"—not unexpectedly since, if it had worked, they wouldn't be attending the seminar—and to the second, "Yes, it's suffered terribly." The bottom line is that bullying, pushing, confronting, and trying to strong-arm anyone into "seeing it your way"—or even calmly but resolutely digging in your heels—will always result in your becoming the enemy and virtually ensuring the two results you want least. The other person will *never* be able to see things your way, and the relationship between you will be seriously damaged, if not entirely broken.

The Change Paradox

Psychologists have discovered that once you stop pushing people to accept your view of things, they'll be more likely to listen to you and change. We call this the change paradox. You may have encountered an everyday version of this paradox commonly called reverse psychology. The concept is simple. When you stop demanding that someone do something your way or admit he is wrong, that person stops defending his position. When you give him what looks like permission to have his own opinion, he feels valued and becomes more open to seeing your point of view, as well as to questioning his own.

Many years ago, before I became a psychologist, I worked as a sales manager for a company that sold solar energy in Arizona. Sure, Arizona had plenty of sun, but the common argument I got from potential customers went something like this: "What am I going to do with solar heat and hot water when I'm trying to cool our house and swimming pool four months of the year!"

"But what about the other eight months?" I would counter. "Besides, there are great tax credits that will offset the blah, blah, blah, blah. . . ." I didn't actually say the "blahs," but in retrospect I am sure that's what my customers heard because I was not absorbing their resistance. Instead, I met their complaint with the counterargument I had learned when I was trained. I was meeting their facts with facts of my own. I was pushing back, rather than listening. As a result, I wasn't good at selling anything until, that is, I learned about the change paradox and the related tactic of absorbing or going with a person's resistance. Here is what the same conversation looked like after I learned this technique:

"What am I going to do with solar heat and hot water when I'm trying to cool our house and swimming pool four months of the year!"

"I see your point. I wouldn't want solar heat during the summer and fall—it's too hot!" I said, going with the resistance. And what do you think would usually happen next? People would become curious. If I wasn't going to argue—if, instead, I agreed with their reasons for not wanting what I was selling—then I must have some other reasons they hadn't thought of. At the very least, they no longer had any reason to resist me and push back. If they didn't then bring it up on their own, I would ask, "Can I tell you why I think it might be worth looking into?" Since I had already neutralized their reason for resisting by agreeing with them, their answer to my question was usually "Yes."

> The change paradox is simple. When you stop demanding that someone admit he is wrong, that person stops defending his position. When you give him what looks like permission to have his own opinion, he feels valued and becomes more open to seeing your point of view, as well as to questioning his own.

Here's another example. I was taking care of my nephew, who was four years old at the time. He was eating his lunch, and I noticed that he was carefully avoiding his vegetables. The chicken nuggets were nearly gone but every single vegetable remained on the plate. So I asked, "Aren't you going to eat your veggies, big guy?"

"No! I don't want them!" he answered, ready for a fight.

"Yeah, I wouldn't want them either. If I were you I wouldn't eat them."

"For reals?" he asked, incredulous.

"For reals. Don't eat them. In fact, I forbid you to eat your veggies. Don't touch them or I'll be mad!" After this small bit of reverse psychology he gave me his most mischievous smile and began to shovel the vegetables into his mouth as fast as he could, while I shouted, "Hey! Stop that! Cut that out!" We both laughed, and although he knew I was using the change paradox on him—not that he knew what to call it—he couldn't help playing along.

Arguing—a Martial Art?

The change paradox is a lot like jujitsu, which is based on never meeting an opponent's blow head-on but instead using his energy to pull, trip, flip, or otherwise direct his momentum until he is in the position you want (standing next to you as an ally with his arm thrown across your shoulder). To accomplish this in an argument rather than on a martial arts mat you have to give three things: your silence, your ear, and your respect.

First, your silence. Stop telling the other person he is wrong. If you are balking at this advice, I ask again: Has repeatedly giving your opinion changed anything in the past? Will repeating it another ten times help? If you think it will, bookmark this page, go do that, and see what happens. Then come back and keep reading.

Silence can indeed be golden. When you are silent you have stopped pushing and the other person doesn't feel the need to push back. When you are silent the other person has a moment to think, to reflect, to wonder what it is you are now thinking. It's something all therapists learn—to be comfortable with silence—because it makes the other person stop, think, and become curious, rather than simply react.

Lend an ear. Really listen to your adversary's point of view and make sure you understand it fully. That sounds easy on the face of it, but when you're angry and you think the other person is dead wrong, it can be very hard to really hear what he's saying because your reflex is to react and counterpunch. But whenever you listen and let the person know he has been heard, the positive effect is immediate. Defenses go down and your opponent is more open to returning the favor.

> You can give respect for another person's point of view without giving up ground.

Convey your respect for his point of view. When I say this, many people wonder how they can do it without suggesting that they agree and are raising a white flag. If you are one of those people, let me assure you right now that LEAP is not what the authors of *Getting to Yes* call "soft negotiating"; it is not about giving up on getting what you need. On the contrary, what you will be giving is your respect for the other person's point of view without giving up ground. It may be as simple as saying, "I can see why you would think that." Or, "I know a lot of people who would agree with you." But regardless of the exact phrasing, you are making a point of saying, "It's reasonable for you to have that point of view." It may not be reasonable for you, but it is for the person you are arguing with and for other people who share similar views. Acknowledging this without being condescending or contrary will open doors.

Respect Makes People Want to Give

Let me approach this concept from a different, far deeper level. To whom are you most willing to give? Let's start with the big giving. For whom do you go out of your way to give your free time? If you are like most people, the answer is the ones you care about most—your loved ones. These are the people to whom you typically give other things as well. Birthday and holiday gifts. Money. And interpersonal gifts, such as patience, the benefit of the doubt, and praise. A timeless but often overlooked truth is that we are far more generous with the people we love than with those we don't. When we love and feel we are loved by one another, we give. You don't need a Ph.D. to understand this fundamental principle of human relations, but it is easy to forget and even easier not to apply in your daily life.

I am not suggesting that you will love all your opponents in every impasse. In some instances you will be arguing or negotiating with a loved one, but in most situations it will be with people who are strangers or business associates. You don't love them; you may not even like them. But that doesn't mean you can't create an experience that will feel a little bit like love to them—even if they would never call it that. What I'm talking about here is communicating your respect, which is not the same as love but a close cousin. Everyone wants to feel respected. Maybe not by everybody all the time, but by most people most of the time. And when someone feels respected, he or she also feels valued. Just as when we feel loved, when we feel respected and valued, we are more apt to give.

> When we feel respected and valued, we are more apt to give.

So, what does it take to feel respected and valued? Do *you* feel respected and valued when someone interrupts you and doesn't appear the least bit interested in what you have to say? How about when someone dismisses your point of view as simple-minded or just plain wrong? When someone has strong-armed you into doing something you don't want to do? Do you feel respected and valued when you are accused of always wanting things your way? How about when someone has suggested, or said outright, that you are either stupid or lying? Of course you don't. But in the heat of an argument or the cold chill of an impasse, we often do these things—by reflex—even if the other person is someone we are very close to and love dearly. And, in those instances, he or she will feel disrespected, unimportant to you, and perhaps worse.

Arguing with Someone You Love

Even when the person we are at an impasse with is a loved one, we often act in unloving ways. LEAP is a way to avoid these unloving, knee-jerk reactions and to convey genuine respect, which, in turn, helps people to feel loved and, therefore, more open to your point of view. Here's an example. Over the years I have received countless notes from LEAP seminar attendees, and among those notes there have been, from time to time, those like the following, which I got from a father in Texas.

"I love my son very much, but I realized, after learning LEAP, that I was not acting like I loved him. For years it was all or nothing for me. Once I started using LEAP I stopped demanding the impossible, and that helped me to stop being so angry. And so did he. We had barely been talking to each other. Now we're close again. Thank you for helping me to show my son that I love him. Thank you for showing me how to have a relationship with him again."

WHEN I FIRST read that note the main point didn't sink in. I was more curious to know if LEAP had helped this man to break the impasse he'd been in with his son. In fact, as he explained later in the note, that did happen, but it wasn't what had motivated him to write to me. What he really wanted to share with me was that LEAP had helped him to show his son he loved him in a circumstance—an impasse of several years' duration—that had previously made it impossible for him to express those feelings. It changed both how he felt about his son— he admitted that for the duration of the impasse he had not been in touch with his own warm feelings—and how his son felt about him.

If you're stuck in the "I'm right, you're wrong" cycle with a loved one and are able to learn some skills that will allow you to get off that merry-go-round and communicate your respect, your relationship will improve, which will, in turn, make it possible to resolve the disagreement.

Giving Causes Change

Giving your silence, your ear, and ultimately your respect will make people feel valued and, in the case of your loved ones, loved. If you want to bring about a change of heart in someone—if you want him to work with you instead of against you in any particular situation—give these things. Let me give you one final example of how this works.

Psychotherapists, who are, after all, in the business of helping people to change, have learned that success depends upon two simple rules. The first is that the alliance, the relationship, has to be one in which the client feels the therapist likes and respects him and is a person he can trust. There are many different forms of psychotherapy, but all studies point to the fundamental importance of the therapeutic alliance as the prerequisite for change—regardless of the form of therapy. The second rule is that when a therapist is working with a difficult client he has to find something about the client he can genuinely respect and like, maybe even admire. The therapist has to value the client. If he can't, he shouldn't be working with that person, because he will fail to express genuine respect, appreciation, and other positive feelings for him. And without these expressions, the therapist will have little or no influence on the client's choices and behavior.

Notice that I said the therapist's feeling for the client must be "genuine." That's important, because LEAP works only when you're being honest and sincere. In fact, learning LEAP will help you to actually *feel* these positive feelings and, once you do, to express them. Having done that, you will find it very easy to stop telling the person with whom you are at an impasse that he is wrong. Instead, you will be able to really listen to his point of view and convey your respect for it. And he, in turn, will be more open to partnering with you because he feels listened to, respected, valued, and in some cases loved.

By using the change paradox—by not pushing your agenda and instead conveying your respect for your opponent's point of view—you accomplish several things at once. You open up your opponent to your point of view, make him interested in giving you something back, and plant the seeds of trust. Let me put it another way. When someone feels you truly respect his point of view, even though you disagree with it, he will begin to trust you more and want to return in kind what you have given him. It is at that point that change can occur.

PART TWO

Learning
to LEAP

4

The Psychology of LEAP

I wanted to change the world. But I have found that the only thing one can be sure of changing is oneself.

—Aldous Huxley

LEAP is based largely on motivational interviewing, an effective form of therapy that helps people in denial about drug and alcohol addiction to lower their defenses and follow their therapists' recommendations. Motivational interviewing starts with the patient's point of view—how he defines the problem and the solution—rather than with the way the doctor *wants* him to see things. Many psychotherapists not trained in this method tell me that LEAP also reminds them of client-centered therapy, which focuses on doctor-patient collaboration rather than taking a "doctor knows best" approach. Both these therapies emphasize the central importance of the alliance between doctor and patient as a prerequisite for change. In other words, they recognize that the relationship is the key to convincing anyone to change. The therapist must listen, empathize with, and respect the patient's point of view if the therapy is to succeed.

> Once the relationship is marked by trust and respect, you are no longer like a lot of hot air and more like the wind in a sailboat's sails—you can move the person where you want him.

If you're wondering what psychotherapy has to do with breaking an impasse, consider this: When you're trying to persuade someone to give you what you need, you—like the psychotherapist—are in the business of helping him to lower his defenses, open up to you, and follow your lead.

LEAP, however, is not just for therapists. It is a set of tools you can use to positively transform a relationship and get what *you* need. Let's start by going over what LEAP stands for.

- **Listen** reflectively.
- **Empathize** with the other person's point of view.
- **Agree** on those goals you share.
- **Partner** on achieving those goals.

When you Listen-Empathize-Agree-Partner, you stop trying to force your adversary to say she is wrong and begin to listen in a new way that conveys genuine understanding, empathy, appreciation, and respect for her point of view, even though you disagree with it. Read the previous sentence again, only this time imagine you are the person on the receiving end. If you felt you were getting these gifts—and they are gifts, really—wouldn't you be more inclined to listen to your adversary's point of view and give something in return? Like the therapies mentioned above, LEAP focuses on transforming the relationship first. Once the relationship is marked by trust and respect, you are no longer like a lot of hot air and more like the wind in a sailboat's sails—you can move the person where you want him.

LEAP to Negotiate

LEAP has a unique role in negotiations. Let me illustrate. The authors of *Getting to Yes* make a distinction between "principled negotiation" and "positional bargaining." Positional bargaining—taking a position and sticking to it—often leads to stalemate, whereas principled negotiation works because it proceeds from a genuine interest in looking at *shared* concerns and arriving at an agreement that is mutually beneficial. But what if you're dealing with a positional bargainer who is not interested in your concerns, shared or not? When you reach a stalemate, how do you get that person to work with you? Most negotiation models assume that, whatever its state of health, the negotiation is active. This is where LEAP is different. Because LEAP understands that sometimes negotiations break down and become inactive (that is to say, reach an impasse), it gives you the tools to motivate your opponent to open his eyes to your shared interests—to move away from "it's my way or yours"—and work with you to find mutually beneficial solutions. It is designed to break the stalemate and bring the person to the table. Take the case of a friend of mine who rents an apartment in New York City, who complained that her landlord was a positional bargainer. The landlord would not budge from his position that she must sign a renewal on her two-year lease on the first of the month or move out. She had just put in a bid to purchase an apartment in another part of the city. The problem was twofold: If the bid was accepted she could not move in immediately, and if it was not, she would need to stay in her current apartment. So she asked her landlord if she could sign a month-to-month agreement rather than the long-term lease she had signed four times over the past eight years. She had read *Getting to Yes* and attended a two-day workshop that taught the negotiating skills she'd read about in the book. The advice had helped her in her job, but, inexplicably, it was not getting her to yes with her landlord. In fact, it was getting her nowhere. He refused to hear her out and repeatedly quoted the one letter he had sent to her saying the issue was "nonnegotiable."

> If you understand your opponent's point of view you can amass the tools to motivate your opponent to open his eyes to your shared interests—to move away from "it's my way or yours"—and work with you to find mutually beneficial solutions.

When she asked my advice, my first question surprised her. I asked what, if anything, her landlord liked about her (I wanted to shift her focus from the outcome to the quality of their relationship). Perplexed, but willing to play along, she thought for a moment and then said, "I've been a good tenant. I don't complain like many other tenants do, and I fixed up my place." I stowed away that little bit of knowledge for the moment and showed her how to use several LEAP tools: reflective listening (listening and then reflecting back what she'd heard to make sure she understood correctly), normalizing (for example, saying she would feel the same way if she was in her landlord's shoes), strategic empathy (empathizing, in this case, with her landlord's feelings about her proposal), asking questions instead of making statements, and, most important in her case, delaying (resisting the temptation to argue her position, and instead listening and following her landlord's lead). I suggested she use these tools to focus on discovering why he was unwilling to negotiate. I told her point-blank to forget about her ultimate goal for the time being. If she couldn't get him to come to the table, all her best arguments and techniques would be like snowflakes falling in the desert—vanishing into thin air before they hit the ground. Their next conversation went something like this:

"I read your letter again and I realized I didn't understand why it is you feel so strongly about the two-year lease. Maybe if you explained it to me I would feel better about it. Can we talk about this?" she asked her landlord, implicitly suggesting she could be convinced to sign the lease.

"Yes. Fine. But you know my position. I can't have you on a month-to-month. I don't do that for anyone."

"Yes, I know that. I just don't understand why you feel so strongly about it. I think we have had a good relationship these past eight years, and I would like to understand your position better before I decide. Would you mind telling me?" she asked again, subtly drawing his attention to his positive feelings for her—to their generally good relationship.

"You have been a good tenant," he admitted, but then went on, "I don't do month-to-month anymore. I did that in the past and I was always left holding the bag. People move out in the winter and I can't rent the apartment—it sits empty."

"I see your point. You could end up losing four or five months' rent if I moved out in the middle of winter. That's the issue, isn't it?" she asked, using reflective listening and turning the conversation away from generalities to her particular circumstance.

"Yes. That's exactly right."

"Well, then, I wouldn't want to do it either, if I were you," she said, normalizing his position. "And it would make me angry if I were left holding the bag," she added, empathizing with how he seemed to feel.

"So then you see my point?" he said more than asked.

Knowing that I wanted her to delay if she was asked this question, she replied, "I'll answer that in a minute, but I'm curious about what happened with the last person to do this to you?"

Delaying before stating your own position or opinion about your opponent's position accomplishes several things (we will come back to this in detail later), but the main benefit is getting the person to repeatedly ask for your opinion. Doing that moves him from being reactive to you to being receptive—it turns him from someone you are playing tennis with to someone to whom you are pitching a baseball. Rather than competing and hitting back your every volley, he is now on your side, catching every pitch (whether or not he thinks they're good pitches). The landlord's question: "So then you see my point?" is actually an invitation to talk about the impasse, something he had thus far been unwilling to do. By delaying rather than jumping at the very first invitation to talk about the ultimate issue (my friend could have immediately said, "No, I don't agree and would like to tell you my ideas about how to handle this"), you will reassure the other person that you are interested in his position and not focused solely on selling your own ideas. Doing that will lower your opponent's defenses, increase his trust, and lead him to become curious about your point of view.

In my friend's case, this one attempt at delaying worked. Her landlord took the bait and began to complain bitterly about a tenant who had taken advantage of him. As he talked, my friend reflected back what he said and normalized it ("I would feel the same way you do"); she empathized with his anger and worry and refrained from injecting her opinion about the ultimate issue. She did not, for example, say things like, "But I would never do that to you." Instead, she let him come to that conclusion himself over the course of their short conversation. In the end, he did hear her out, and he learned, among other things, that she had a friend who was very interested in taking over the apartment whenever she vacated. It was no guarantee, but that fact, together with his feeling that my friend truly appreciated his position, increased his trust and willingness to explore their shared interests. This one conversation reminded him of his positive feelings for her and demonstrated to him that she appreciated and respected his position. In the end, he let her sign a month-to-month lease with a verbal agreement—which he apparently trusted—that she would do everything in her power to give him more than thirty days' notice and to help him find a new tenant.

Other popular negotiation techniques, like those described in *Getting to Yes*, often fail because the relationship has not been primed. One or both negotiators are largely uninterested in what the other has to say because there is little trust and much defensiveness between them. No negotiation technique is going to work in that situation because the person with whom you want to negotiate has turned a deaf ear. In the example above, my friend used several LEAP tools not only to bring her landlord to the table—a place he had previously been unwilling to go—but also, once he was there, to lower his defenses and increase his trust in her. Ultimately, she was able to use the negotiation techniques she knew, along with other LEAP tools you will be learning about, to arrive at an agreement that satisfied their shared interests. She needed the flexibility and her landlord needed to feel secure. In the end, they both got what they ultimately needed.

How to Find the Right Tool and Use It Effectively

Most of the LEAP tools you'll be acquiring will already look familiar—at least at first glance. Among the core tools are listening reflectively, empathizing strategically, identifying areas of agreement and shared interests, normalizing your opponent's position, delaying giving your opinion, never giving your opinion unless it has been asked for repeatedly, and giving the other person a way to save face. You may have used some, if not all of them, before. And in those instances you probably had some success and may have wondered exactly how that happened. Here you will learn to use these techniques, and others, systematically and purposefully. And when you do, you will suceed much more often and understand why you did.

> LEAP takes no more time than what you are already doing, and delaying giving your opinion does not mean you never give it— only that you wait for the moment when it will be heard and heeded.

At this point, however, you may already be experiencing some of the common forms of resistance I have encountered over the years: "I don't have time for this." "If I listen and empathize without reminding the other person of my position he will assume he's won." "It sounds manipulative; the other person is going to see right through me." Although I will address each of these arguments in more detail later, let me reassure you right now that LEAP takes no more time than what you are already doing, and delaying giving your opinion does not mean you never give it—only that you wait for the moment when it will be heard and heeded. And finally, LEAP is not in any way dishonest. In fact, if you feel like you are lying or manipulating, you are not doing LEAP. What you're aiming for is honestly becoming curious about your opponent's point of view and the reasons for it. Even though you may not agree with much or anything she says, you can come to understand and appreciate her experience. Communicating that understanding and appreciation—if not respect—will transform you and the other person from adversaries into allies (if only in a limited way), and this change in your relationship will make you far more persuasive than you were when you started.

LEAP will help you find the tools you need, dust them off, and store them in a place where they'll always be handy. It will also help you to decide which tool will be most effective in which situation.

I remember using strategic empathy, which was the wrong tool to use at the time, with my thirteen-year-old nephew who had come to live with me for the summer. We were arguing about whether he could spend the night with a friend I had never met and he had known for only a day. When I told him my final answer was no, he sulked and barely spoke to me for the next hour. Even though I had gotten what I wanted—using my superior authority in this situation (I was the adult and he was the child)—our relationship was suffering. I wanted to talk further so we could both feel better about the outcome. I wanted an opportunity to express my understanding of why he was angry and respect that. Feeling confident in my ability to do this, I approached him, empathetically saying, "I'm sorry you're angry about this."

"I'm not angry!" he practically shouted, then added, "You're not my therapist!" You, too, may encounter a similar reaction when you start to use LEAP: "You're talking like a therapist." Had I first used reflective listening, I have no doubt I could have expressed my empathy effectively. But because I rushed to empathy (used the wrong tool at the wrong time), I momentarily made matters worse. I quickly recovered, however, and using the more appropriate LEAP tool (reflective listening), I said flatly, "I sound like a therapist?"

"Yeah, you're not my therapist."

"You're right. I'm not. Sorry about that. Did that piss you off?" I asked, making another attempt at empathy now that I had successfully reflected back his new complaint about me.

"It's weird when you do that."

"I can see why it's weird—I guess a lot of people would feel the same way," I said nondefensively, thereby normalizing his feelings. "Can we talk about the sleepover?" I asked, now more confident that, because of our momentary reconnection, he would be willing to do that. He said yes, and I was able not only to diffuse his anger but also to suggest that I meet his new friend and his parents and that we plan a sleepover for later in the week. This might seem like a lot of effort for a situation in which I had already won the argument, but, in fact, it took no more than five minutes, and transformed the rest of our evening from tension and sulking to enjoying each other's company and a movie.

How Is As Important As *What*

Whenever you acquire a new tool, you need to learn how to use it properly. For example, if you're using a hammer for the first time, you have to get a feel for how hard to strike the nail so that it sinks in but doesn't bend. LEAP will show you how to use the tools you acquire so you don't sound like a therapist or fake. In that sense, mastering LEAP is as much about process as content. For example, a friend told me about a colleague who had attended a seminar on team building because morale among his employees was low. This colleague was not well liked by his employees before he attended the seminar, and things didn't improve much afterward. As my friend explained it, "After the seminar he used to squeeze people's shoulders or literally pat them on the back after asking them to do something. It was obviously a technique he had learned about, but it didn't change morale because he didn't know how to use it." The reason, he explained, was that his colleague hadn't really connected with the person to whom he was giving the orders. When using LEAP, you will learn much about the person you are at an impasse with, and in the process you will come to appreciate his position even if you do not agree with it. As a result, you will genuinely connect with him—as I ultimately did with my nephew and my friend did with her landlord. If nothing else, he will feel understood, and if you are systematic in your use of LEAP there's a very good chance he will feel respected and trusting. If you can achieve this, a squeeze on the shoulder may be just the thing.

The moral of the shoulder-squeezing story is that acquiring new tools or techniques is never enough. You have to know how to use them (and I am not talking about how much pressure to put into the shoulder squeeze). The misguided manager in this story did not understand or embrace the principle underlying the technique. If he had, he would have known how to use it. Although I wasn't at that seminar, I assume the principle being taught was that expressions of appreciation are motivating and can improve morale. But if there is no connection and trust, a shoulder squeeze or pat on the back will never feel genuine—you might even get slapped with a sexual harassment claim!

The nearly magical thing about LEAP is that it opens the user to more positive feelings about the person with whom he or she is arguing. If you can feel positively about the person with whom you are at an impasse, even in a limited way, you will be authentic when you listen, empathize, agree, partner, and make use of the other tools LEAP provides. You will lower their defenses, open them up to you, and create a connection.

5

Before You LEAP—
Stop and Look Both Ways

You can't shake hands with a clenched fist.

—Mahatma Gandhi

It wasn't too long ago that, in the heat of a highly charged moment, I almost failed to practice what I preach. Luckily, I was able to catch myself and save the situation from deteriorating beyond repair.

What happened was this. My mother was in the intensive care unit of a hospital in another state halfway across the country, and I was trying to learn everything I could about her condition and treatment so I could be certain everything she needed was being done. I'd already called the hospital and asked that the entire contents of her chart be faxed to me. Legally, I was entitled to this information because I had my mother's medical power of attorney, and the fax arrived in due course. When I went through the records, however, I discovered that two days' worth of crucial progress notes were missing, so I called again to ask that the missing portion be faxed to me.

This time I spoke to a nurse on the ICU. I introduced myself using my "doctor" title, explained the situation, and asked her to fax me the notes. Her immediate response was that the HIPAA (Health Insurance Portability and Accountability Act) regulations did not allow her to do that, and, what is more, that whoever had sent me the previous fax had no right to have done it. Being a doctor, I should have known better and was wrong to even ask.

My instinctive reaction was to become angry and arrogant. "I sat on the medical review committee at Columbia University. I know all about HIPAA, and you're wrong. You can fax the information to me because I have my mother's medical power of attorney." In that one thoughtless moment I made three mistakes. I told the nurse, in effect, that she was stupid; I told her I was more expert than she; and I allowed my anger to blind me to everything I knew about how I *should* be handling the situation. My feeling brain had overcome my thinking brain, which had apparently fallen asleep at the wheel, and things started to go downhill fast.

"I've just gone through this with another patient," she said, "and our HIPAA officer told me I never should have done it." Now she was pulling in her own expert to counter my claim that I was more expert than she. She was defensive, her voice was becoming shrill, and the argument was escalating. "Whoever faxed you those notes was wrong," she went on. "Who did it?"

At that point we were no longer arguing about my mother's medical chart, and the nurse was actually asking me to rat on my source. I had made her more defensive than she was originally, and I could see that we'd reached an impasse. I wasn't getting anything from this woman, certainly not what I needed. It wouldn't do me any good to curse her out, which is where I was headed, and if I hung up on her, I'd never get those records. In fact, she might make things more difficult for me in the future if she decided to put a note in the chart saying that I'd been abusive to her on the phone.

So I took a deep breath and started again, with an apology. "I'm really sorry," I said, honestly feeling bad about how quickly the argument had escalated even though I was not yet feeling much empathy for her experience. "So, as I understand it, the problem you have is that your hands are tied. You've been told by your HIPAA officer that you can't do this. You did it once before and you got in trouble for it. That's your predicament, right?"

"Yes. That's exactly the problem," she answered, now sounding more nervous than angry.

"If I were you, I would be nervous about faxing anything ever again," I said, taking a stab at empathy and normalizing her reaction—making a connection between us.

"Well, I'm far from comfortable," she admitted.

Once she could hear that I was **listening** to her, she let slip another feeling that had been hidden by her anger—anxiety. When I realized she was anxious, I actually started to feel a little genuine **empathy** and said, "Then this must be very frustrating for you." Even I was amazed by how quickly her tone softened. "Yes," she said. "It certainly is."

"Well, I'm just trying to help my mother, which is, I'm sure, what you want to do, too." Since she was a nurse, I had to assume that she really did care about her patients, so we could **agree** that we had caring for my mother in common.

Then, without waiting for her response, I asked, "What would you do if you were in my shoes? Do you have any suggestions?" By asking her opinion, I was ceding power to her instead of trying to strong-arm her into submission, and I was asking her to find a way to **partner** with me in our common quest to do what was best for my mother. By listening, empathizing, and staking out an area of agreement I had transformed our interaction from that of two bulls locking horns to that of a cowboy on horseback herding the wayward bull back home.

> "What would you do if you were in my shoes? Do you have any suggestions?" By asking her opinion, I was ceding power to her instead of trying to strong-arm her into submission, and I was asking her to find a way to *partner* with me.

She was silent for a moment, and I could tell that she, too, was stepping back and calming down. Then she said, "You know what, let me look through the chart and see what's in there for those two days."

And at that point, without my asking, she started reading out loud from the chart. She spent the next fifteen minutes reading me word for word exactly what was written for the two missing days. There were, in fact, some surprising and alarming details about what had happened during this time that concerned us both. At the end of the conversation she also gave me the direct-dial number of the HIPAA officer and suggested I call him directly. She volunteered the pager numbers of two doctors I'd been unable to reach by phone, told me what time they'd be doing rounds again, and promised to have a doctor call me as soon as they were finished—a promise she kept. When I hung up the phone I had a smile on my face and warm, positive feelings for this woman. I am sure she sensed that shift in my feelings about her soon after I broke the "I'm right, you're wrong" cycle and began to use LEAP because she ended the call by saying, "Feel free to call me back if there's anything I can do."

Notice that when the argument began what I thought I needed was a fax. And when the nurse told me she couldn't send it (which, incidentally, is not true—see, I still think I was right and she was wrong!), I got so angry I became fixated on *making* her send it to me. Not only would I never have been able to do that, but once I took a step back and cooled off I was able to see it wasn't really the fax I needed at all— it was the information in my mother's chart. Sure, I *wanted* the fax, but what I *needed* was to learn what was written on the missing pages. If I hadn't been able to get my own anger under control, I'd never have been able to diffuse hers or create the relationship with her that ultimately allowed her to *want* to find a way to help me get what I needed. I needed information and what I ultimately realized was that it made no difference whether I received it via fax, letter, telephone, telegraph, or smoke signals. In the end, that nurse and I became partners with the common goal of finding a way to help my mother.

This particular exchange took place in a medical context. I'm a doctor, I was talking to a nurse, and we were arguing about my mother's medical records. But the same kind of exchange might just as easily occur between you and a store clerk or an airline ticket agent. Maybe you want a cash refund for a sweater you received as a gift but you don't have the receipt, so the clerk can only issue a store credit. Screaming that it's a gift and the clerk is an idiot will not, I guarantee you, get you your money back. In fact, all you'll get is elevated blood pressure and an entrenched adversary. But if you acknowledge that the clerk has to follow store policy, you will allow him to be right and open the door to his finding a way to get you what you need—because he will want to. Or maybe you need to convince the ticket agent not to bump you from an overbooked flight for which you are holding a confirmed reservation. Banging on the counter and letting her know about the meeting in Chicago that can't possibly take place without you isn't going to cut it. But commiserating with her dilemma and asking her what she would do in your place might just get her to find you a seat in business class.

Take the Temperature of the Argument

When you're seeing red, the fire in your eyes blinds you to everything else. In addition, your ears are probably ringing so you can't even hear what the other person is saying. And the same, I assure you, is true for the person with whom you are arguing. Getting what you need, therefore, depends, first of all, on knowing when you or the other person is getting too angry or defensive.

You may not always be in the position to pick and choose just the right moment to argue. What you need to be aware of, then, is when the argument is getting too overheated so you can take a time-out, even if it's only a few seconds, and give the person you're arguing with time to do the same.

> A well-placed apology can give you and the person you're arguing with time to stop and think about the direction things are going.

In my conversation with the nurse it really didn't take very long, once I saw the warning signs. When I caught myself pulling rank and found myself thinking, "What a bitch!" I literally stopped talking and took a deep breath. Then I quickly apologized, even though I wasn't feeling apologetic about what I wanted. But, like the well-trained waiter who apologizes when a mistake has been made without blaming himself or anyone else, I *was* sorry that my request had devolved into a toxic argument.

Even if you are not yet feeling remorse for what you have just said, a well-placed apology—an expression of sorrow that an impasse has been reached—can give you and the person you're arguing with time to stop and think about the direction things are going. It is also a way for you to help the other person save face—which usually eliminates his defensiveness. Sometimes, however, it can take a while longer for the other person to let go of his defenses and be ready to hear you, so part of what you need to be doing at all times is to monitor the temperature of the exchange, which will allow you to know when he's no longer emotionally deaf, dumb, and blind and will be receptive to what you have to say.

Know When It's Too Hot Not to Cool Down

What if you got into your car, turned the key in the ignition, and saw the bright red temperature gauge light up on the dash—would you ignore the warning and drive off anyway? Would you proceed if you also saw steam snaking up from under the hood? What if the engine started to make loud knocking sounds? Would you still drive on?

Cars come equipped with thermostats that constantly monitor engine temperature, because when the motor gets too hot the engine will soon stop working and serious damage will be done. When the engine temperature light comes on—one of my brothers, who is a mechanic, calls it the idiot light because you would have to be an idiot to ignore it—you need to stop driving, turn off the car, and let the engine cool down. You do this for two reasons: to prevent further damage and to fix the problem. Fortunately, the emotional temperature of an argument can also be monitored, and for the same reasons. But there isn't any idiot light for arguments, so you need to pay attention to the signals that let you know when you and/or the other person are overheating. You will know it's time to cool off when:

You

- find yourself interrupting the other person;
- don't feel listened to or heard by the other;
- engage in name-calling, either directly or by implication, letting the other person know you think he's a liar, stubborn, a fool, a jerk, or all of the above;
- bring up issues that have nothing to do with the argument of the moment (which I call kitchen-sinking it);
- have the argument in front of other people (in public, in front of children, employees, and so on).

The other person

- interrupts you;
- says you're not listening to him;
- calls you names (as above).

If you're constantly interrupting one another, neither of you is really interested in listening to the other and you're certainly not hearing what the other person has to say. What are you thinking and feeling when someone interrupts you? If you are like most people, you are still thinking about what you were about to say, not listening, and you're probably getting irritated. You're getting heated.

If someone tells you, "You're not listening!" or "No, that's not what I said!" he's right and you're wrong. Maybe not objectively, but that's the experience he's having, and that's all you have to work with. Until you correct his misconception (if he was in fact wrong and you were listening) or do a better job of listening, he will hold a little grudge against you and not feel any obligation to listen any further to your arguments. How do you feel when you're arguing with someone who you think is not listening to you?

If you've sunk so low that you're calling the other person names, you're communicating, whether you mean to or not, that you're not remotely interested in hearing anything he might have to say (except, of course, that you're right). And worse still, you have made the other person feel defensive, thereby eclipsing anything you say after the insult.

If you've gotten to the point of reminding him of past petty indiscretions—such as, "And last Tuesday you came to the meeting late . . ."—he will probably become even more defensive because he now feels he has to start defending himself on a whole new battlefront. Therefore, all you'll have accomplished is to escalate the skirmish into an out-and-out war.

> When arguments are public we become more focused on saving face and more sensitive to feeling humiliated. And when that happens we're unlikely to get what we need.

And if you are having the argument in front of other people, you will both be more defensive than you would be if you were going at it one-on-one. When arguments are public we become more focused on saving face and more sensitive to feeling humiliated. You will also run the risk of being tempted to draw the witnesses into the argument, a tactic that almost never works to break an impasse. As soon as you pull in reinforcements ("Anne, you agree with me, don't you?" "I sure do," Anne answers), your opponent will pull in his ("Oh yeah? Well, Gary, Ben, and Alex all agree with me!"). And arguing in front of children is often one of the most obvious and easily recognized warning signs that the argument has become too hot.

If one or more of these things is happening—if you or the other person is interrupting, feeling unheard, name-calling, kitchen-sinking, or arguing in front of other people—the idiot light is on, steam is escaping from under the hood, the engine is knocking loudly, and if you don't stop soon the engine will seize up.

Collateral Damage

When you wage war in a populated area (and, in the case of toxic arguments, that means in front of even one other person), innocent bystanders are likely to get hurt. This is true whether the impasse is between two members of a family, business partners, friends, or even two strangers. And when that happens, it complicates the argument and makes the impasse harder to break.

Among the most obvious examples of this is when parents argue in front of children. Melinda was arguing with Tim about whether he spent enough time at home. She felt he spent more time than he needed to at work and that, as a result, the family was being neglected. They were stuck at an impasse: Melinda argued that Tim didn't need to work on the weekends, and Tim told her she was wrong and didn't know what she was talking about. When I spoke with them, they told me their arguments seemed to get nowhere; they just went round and round. Instead of having a sober discussion aimed at identifying and satisfying their shared interests, the arguments became heated and they were stuck. Their last go-around had occurred in front of their six-year-old son, Dylan, who was sitting at the kitchen counter drawing and "not listening." Suddenly, at the top of his lungs, Dylan yelled, "Da da, da da, ba ba mama, da da, ba ba, pow!"

Stopping herself in mid-sentence, Melinda turned to her son and shouted, "Dylan! You're not a baby. Stop talking baby talk."

"Da da, da da, mama, pow-pow-pow!"

"All right, D, that's enough. You heard your mother," Tim said, trying to be helpful.

Eyebrows raised, Melinda jumped in. "Don't bother, Tim. I deal with him all week and on weekends, so don't suddenly try to act like you're a parent!"

"Fine. I won't. I'll be at the office," Tim retorted, storming out.

In this instance Melinda didn't heed the warning signs that things were getting too hot (kitchen-sinking and name-calling), and neither she nor Tim, in the moment, realized that arguing in front of their son was making matters worse. When I asked them about this later they both said that Dylan's presence had amplified their reactions. Melinda felt angrier because she saw him playing alone and having to listen to his parents argue when she knew he missed his father and would rather have been playing with him. She blamed Tim for the argument, for being stubborn. Tim felt much more defensive with his son there.

He felt he was answering his wife's challenges while simultaneously trying to defend himself to his son. It felt more humiliating. Ironically, Dylan's presence made them both feel less like partners than if they had been talking alone.

Ask yourself whether arguing in front of that person made you (or your adversary) feel angrier, defensive, or humiliated.

After Tim stormed out Melinda tried to talk to Dylan about what had happened, but he refused to listen, saying several times, "I don't want to talk about it" and "You're mean." That night, after reading his son a bedtime story, Tim apologized to Dylan for having argued in front of him. Dylan's response was to ask, "Why do you make Mommy cry?" Later, when Tim was getting into bed with his wife, he told her what Dylan had said and Melinda recounted her own failed attempt to talk with him about the argument. At that point they both realized that whenever either of them tried to talk to him, Dylan would take the other's side. They understood they had put him in the middle, and neither of them wanted to do that—this was something they could agree on.

Think back on the last time you had a toxic overheated argument in front of a third party. Try to replay the argument while standing in the bystander's shoes. If the bystander is a coworker, what did your argument do to his or her morale? Did this person feel he needed to choose sides? What price was paid? And ask yourself whether arguing in front of that person made you (or your adversary) feel angrier, defensive, or humiliated.

Wake Up Your Thinking Brain

Despite the way it may sound, I am *not* asking you to instantly stop being angry or frustrated or to just "get over" whatever other emotion has been driving your behavior. Like Melinda and Tim, you're human, not a robot, and you probably can't just stop being angry by throwing a switch. That's why I'm going to give you some tools for tipping the balance so that your thinking brain can retake control of your emotional brain. But whether or not you are immediately successful at using these strategies, whether or not you calm down, you can still change how you act in response to your emotions so you avoid the very common mistakes that cause people to throw fuel on the fire instead of dousing the flames. And, as you change your behavior by acting *as if* you were less angry, you'll discover that your anger will usually diminish all on its own.

Stop, Look, and Listen: When you're angry, stop, look at the other person, and listen to see if he is angry, too. What you do next can either throw fuel on the fire and take you further from what you want, or it can lower both your temperatures so you are able to find common ground.

At this point you might be thinking, "Okay, maybe I can control how I react to my own emotional state, but I have no control over the other person's reactions." In fact you do. And, perhaps most interesting of all, you'll discover that as you act less angry and more interested in the other person's point of view, her anger will also diminish. The effect is synergistic. So as much as you might want to push that other person's buttons—and you certainly will—what you need to do is bite your tongue, swallow those incendiary words, and get curious about her perspective.

Throw Water on the Fire

Contrary to what you may be thinking, it's not really so difficult to diffuse another person's anger. Law enforcement officers who are specially trained members of Crisis Intervention Teams (CITs) do it all the time when they walk into an unknown situation and a perfect stranger is ranting and raving. In contrast to the majority of police officers, those who are CIT-trained are taught to put out their hands, palms up, and say, "Tell me what's going on here." That's it. No "Calm down, buddy," no "Hands on your head," just "Tell me what's going on." By saying that, what they're actually conveying is, "I'm here to listen and I want to know your point of view." That's really what most people want; they want to know you're listening to them and considering their point of view. And once they feel that you are, it's very hard for them to feel angry or defensive.

Notice I didn't say "agreeing with" their point of view; by considering it, however, you're showing them respect—you are honoring it. Think about how you feel when you're not being listened to or when you think your point of view is being insulted. If you're like me, you get angry and stop listening.

Turn Down the Heat

When your biological alarm system goes off, your nervous system goes on automatic. But if you can use your thinking brain long enough, you can shut down the feeling brain and regain control. You already have your own strategies for calming yourself down when you're overheated. We all do. But I'm going to give you three more. Since I am a confessed acronym addict—acronyms help me to memorize things I want to remember—here is another one.

When you get sucked into an impasse and are angry, I want you to take a gamble on doing things differently and BET:

- Breathe
- Exit
- Think

Breathe: When your amygdala takes control of your brain chemistry, your breathing is shallow and fast. As it turns out, however, simply taking deep, slow breaths and exhaling fully (you may have learned this in your birthing classes if you've had a baby) will activate the inhibitory circuits that return your neural chemistry to a calmer state, removing the tunnel vision and allowing you to see the bigger picture.

When you feel frustrated and locked into wanting your adversary to wave the white flag or he is accusing you of being wrong, remember to take deep, slow breaths from your abdomen and exhale fully. Take just three and you will find it helps. The other person won't even know you are doing it because he too will be seeing red. Try it and see if you feel any different. What do you have to lose?

Exit: Next, you need to get out of the situation that has triggered your brain's alarm system. You need to figuratively, and sometimes literally, walk away from the impasse. But like most things having to do with human relations, *how* you do this also makes a big difference. When Tim stormed out of the kitchen during his argument with Melinda, he made her angrier, not calmer. And because his exit followed immediately upon Melinda's accusing him of being a bad parent, he stewed rather than cooled down.

Walking away figuratively rather than literally is usually easier, but you have to have enough presence of mind to pull it off. The example I gave of the waiter who apologized and took a new order is an example of what I am talking about. The potential impasse she avoided had started with her customer's telling her she'd made a mistake. The server believed she was right, but rather than return the volley with, "No. I got the order right," she took the nearest exit. She apologized and said, in effect, let's fix this.

Sometimes, when we are too angry, we can't think of the words that will lead to that exit, or, even if we do, the other person is not making it easy for us to leave the impasse. What then? Sometimes we simply have to literally walk away or hang up the phone. Of course, if you slam the door on your way out or slam down the receiver, you will only make things worse. What you need to do instead is give fair warning, or, better yet, if you are already breathing more slowly and have the presence of mind, ask permission by saying something like, "Would you mind if we finish this later?" Asking permission to finish the argument later is a powerful tool because you are giving the other person a moment of control. When you say something like, "If it's okay with you, I would like to stop talking right now and finish this later because I want to calm down," you are asking for a favor and admitting to being overheated and not at your best. This creates a connection between you and the person you are fighting with. At the very least, the person bestowing the favor will feel "one up"—gain the dignity that comes from being the one who bestows the favor—which will reduce his anger and defensiveness. It is yet another way to help someone save face.

> Asking permission to finish the argument later is a powerful tool because you are giving the other person a moment of control.

Although I have found this strategy to be extremely effective, the other person might not yet be willing to do you a favor. If the response you get to your request is, "No, I want to finish this right now!" you might have to go a step further. First of all, don't take the bait, because, in that moment, you will both be too angry to get anything accomplished. Remember, the whole point of this strategy is to place some distance between you and the trigger that's firing up your feeling brain so you will be able to calm down and use the tools you are now acquiring to get what you need. What you should do, therefore, is apologize and end the conversation (if only for two minutes, as in, "I will call you right back").

If you're arguing with someone you are close to, you can say, "I'm sorry, I have to calm down, but I promise I'll finish this later." By doing that, you are not blaming the other person; rather, you are letting him know *you* are the one who needs to calm down and you are asking his permission to come back to the issue later. If it is a stranger or business associate, such self-disclosure might be awkward, in which case you can make an excuse. If you're on the phone you can say, "I am sorry, I have another call I have to take. Can I call you right back?" If the impasse is face-to-face, simply say, "There's an important call I have to make. Can I come back in a moment and finish this?" And if that feels too dishonest, let me suggest that you do, indeed, have a very important call to make—you need to call upon your frontal lobes!

Just remember always to follow the excuse with an assurance that you will get right back to the person and finish the argument.

Think: This is the easiest of the three BET tactics, and you may find that it's the one you use first. To see how it works, picture yourself following a narrow path through the woods. Right in front of you is a towering brick wall you keep walking into like a mindless windup toy. Each time you take a few steps forward, you slam into the wall, bounce back, march forward, again hit the wall, bounce back, and start forward again. See it in your mind's eye. What does this image say to you? It's telling you that you are not making any headway and that, no matter how many times you try, you are powerless to move forward. When you see that simple truth, it will be far easier to breathe and exit the impasse.

> Winning is not about hearing the other person say, "You're right." It's about getting him to agree to act in ways that get you what you really need, even when he doesn't agree with you.

A final word. Don't fret if, after reading this chapter, you still fall into the tunnel-vision trap. It's a natural reflex. You can't help it any more than I or anyone else. All you can do is get better at knowing when it happens—noticing when the warning light flashes so you can stop, take a short step back, and ask yourself, "What's the big picture here? What is it I really need?" Do you want your kid to agree that vegetables are good for him or do you want him to eat his vegetables? Do you want the plumber to admit he installed your dishwasher wrong or do you want your dishwasher fixed? Do you want to make the sale or have your customer agree with you that the competition's product is inferior? Do you want your boss to acknowledge you're the most talented member of the team—not that this wouldn't be nice—or do you want a raise and more vacation time? I think you get the point.

What you ought to be doing instead of focusing myopically on your rightness is to stop hitting your head against the brick wall like some mindless windup toy or primitive reptile, step back, and identify your real goal. Winning is not about hearing the other person say, "You're right." It's about getting him to agree to act in ways that get you what you really need, even when he doesn't agree with you. In those terms, it becomes clear that whether he *ever* agrees with you is totally immaterial. In fact, getting stuck on hearing "You're right" is one of the surest ways there is to turn an argument into a toxic power struggle that results in a broken relationship and no one's winning anything.

Remember the Reason You're Doing This

I'm not a saint, and I don't expect you to be one either. I was really angry when I was talking to that nurse, but I was also aware that I *needed something from her*—something that was important to me. And because I needed something, I needed to create a positive working relationship with her, at least for the length of that phone call. What I did was totally pragmatic. I didn't think to myself, "Xavier, stop being angry." What I did was take a couple of deep breaths and think, "Xavier, wait a minute, you need something from this woman and if you keep this up, you're never going to get it."

If I hadn't needed anything, I may have given in to my basest instincts and at least had the momentary satisfaction of cursing her out and hanging up on her—which is more or less exactly what I did when someone stole my parking space a few weeks ago. I'd pulled up to the car in front of the space and was backing in when a guy in a much smaller car snuck up behind me and moved into *my* space going forward. I got out of my car, motioned for him to roll down his window so we could talk—which he refused to do—and proceeded to shout so he could hear, "Hey, that was my spot! I was here first." At that point, the other guy made a classic rude gesture, which I returned, along with a few well-chosen insults. In that situation I took the bait and responded in kind. I suppose not much was lost in that interaction because I probably wasn't going to get my space back no matter what I said. But I do think I missed an opportunity to try, even though the odds were against me. I know for sure I lost the next fifteen minutes or so consumed in anger.

The point here is that LEAP isn't something you're going to be engaging in just because you can or because you want to be considered for sainthood. It's a method you'll be using because you've got your eye on the prize, so to speak, and this is a way for you to get what you need. And what you need may be more than a concession from the person on the other side of the argument. It may also be feeling good about yourself and being able to let go of a disagreement you just had with someone. If you can keep that in mind, it might just help you to BET on your ability to act more like the great persuader and less like the Hulk.

6

Listen—in Order to Disarm

He who cannot be a good follower cannot be a good leader.

—Aristotle

Fools talk, cowards are silent, wise men listen.

—Carlos Ruiz Zafón

When I was five years old I wanted to be Batman. Superman, Spider-Man, and the Hulk were also appealing, but for me they were all a distant second to Batman. It wasn't his mask and ears—which I remember thinking looked goofy—it was that amazing Bat Utility Belt. I had to have a Batman costume for Halloween; nothing else would do. I still remember how I felt when I strapped on that belt for the first time. I could conquer all evil, set things right, and live to tell the tale. I had power.

The best thing about Batman was that he was a regular person. He did not have superpowers. It was his tool belt—and that's really all it was—that set him apart from mere mortals. There were many high-tech tools in that belt, but my favorite was the grappling hook attached to a dental-floss-thin rope that he used to walk up the sides of buildings. With those tools, there was no wall he could not climb, no obstacle he could not overcome. There was no enemy he could not beat.

I want you to imagine that you, too, have a tool belt. It can be made of any material you want. It can be stylish like Dolce & Gabbana or purely functional-looking like Craftsman. Imagine it is empty. Loops, hooks, and pockets all lay open and ready to receive the tools you will need to break an impasse. I'm going to provide you with the tools to fill that belt. They will serve you well, but you'll have to practice using them. I'm sure the very first time Batman threw his grappling hook over a wall, it missed its mark and fell back, nearly hitting the Caped Crusader. Even he had to practice before he became proficient at using the tools in his belt.

Reflective Listening

"In prattling Paris it was noted that [Benjamin] Franklin did something extraordinary. He listened. And any word that did escape his lips sped instantly around the kingdom," writes Stacy Schiff in her biography, *A Great Improvisation*.

It's a fundamental rule of negotiation that if you want someone to consider your point of view, you need to make sure he feels you've seriously considered his. And it's an equally fundamental rule of relationships that we all want to feel heard and respected.

So listening and making sure you understand your opponent's position is key. In fact, it is the cornerstone of the LEAP method. Without this tool in your tool belt, you will almost certainly fail.

We all know how to listen. No one needs to buy a book to learn how to listen. But *reflective* listening is something very different from ordinary listening.

Most people have heard the words "just shut up and listen" at least once in their lives. Reflective listening, however, requires that the listener also talk, or, more specifically, ask questions. The sole purpose of reflective listening is for the listener to understand what the other person is trying to say and then reflect her understanding back without any comment or controversy. It's an active process in which your role as the listener is to let the other person know you're trying to get it right. When you're doing that, you'll need to ask questions simply to confirm that what you *think* the other person is saying is, in fact, what he intended. If you're doing it right, you will sound a lot like a journalist conducting an interview. A journalist doesn't respond to what was just said, he doesn't say, "I think you've got that wrong" or express any personal feelings. A journalist relies entirely on the interviewee's willingness to talk. To inspire that willingness there needs to be at least a modicum of trust. And one way to create that trust is to have the other person believe you are really trying to understand his perspective.

If you want to get people talking freely, you need to learn the value of asking if you got it right—if you understood them correctly—without passing any judgment on what they have to say. Amazingly enough, when you use reflective listening you'll discover that as soon as the other person believes you really *want* to hear what he has to say, that you are truly trying to understand his point of view, he will be disarmed and begin to trust you. This is a major reason that investigative journalists are so successful at getting people to talk to them on air, even when it is obviously not in their best interest.

> When you use reflective listening you'll discover that as soon as the other person believes you really *want* to hear what he has to say, that you are truly trying to understand his point of view, he will be disarmed and begin to trust you.

Questions create connections and give your opponent some measure of control. Questions also convey respect. Think about the language one uses when addressing a judge or a king: "If it please the court . . ." "May I approach . . ." I'm not suggesting you treat the person you're arguing with like royalty; I am just making the point that questions can do much more than query.

Questions are also useful because they say you assume nothing. Not even how the other person feels. If you've ever had the experience of saying to someone, "You sound angry," only to have them bark back at you, "I'm not angry!!!" you will understand the value of asking the question first.

To illustrate how well this works, let's look at two sisters, Laura, who was married with children, and her younger sister Carol, who was single and lived alone. They had recently argued over plans they were trying to make together for a surprise anniversary party for their parents. The plans got quickly stalled when they couldn't agree on a date (their parents already had plans for the actual anniversary date). Carol told me that the discussion of dates quickly became heated, devolved into name-calling, and ended before it had even started. She confessed she was leaning toward giving in to her older sister once again. For Carol, the issue was this: Laura felt her schedule should always trump her single sister's schedule because Laura had "a husband and kids to consider." Carol, a highly successful television producer with a grueling schedule and relentless deadlines to meet, didn't agree that Laura's schedule should always rule the day. All she was asking was for Laura to consider her schedule—to just ask Carol when she was free—instead of announcing the dates they could have the party. "I told her she was selfish and self-centered," Carol told me when recounting this first conversation. "I mean, she deserved it! How dare she just announce, 'We can have the party on either the seventh or the eighth.' What a bitch! It's been like this my whole life."

I asked her to describe the conversation in more detail, and this is more or less how it went.

Laura began, "This is such a crazy time of year with school not being out yet and their exams and dance classes; I don't know how I'm going to make it through the month without a nervous breakdown! So looking at my schedule, it looks like we can have the party on either the seventh or the eighth."

"I can't make either of those dates. I have two pieces airing that week. Can't we do it the week before, or better yet, the week after?" Carol asked.

"No. You know we're taking the girls to Maine on the fifteenth, and before is just too hectic. You'll just have to squeeze Mom and Dad in. Family is more important. At least it should be."

"What are you saying? You're the one who is not giving me dates I can work with. You're the one who is putting your schedule ahead of our family!"

"No. I have a family and I am putting family first," Laura said smugly.

"You selfish, self-centered bitch!" Carol said, incredulous.

I asked her what happened next; Carol confessed, "The next thing she heard was the dial tone."

A couple of things stood out for me as Carol described the exchange. First, she did not reflect back her sister's statement or show any appreciation for her sister's situation. Instead, she reacted to what she heard defensively and angrily, focusing on what she wanted to hear rather than what she actually heard. Second, as she told me the story, she kept sounding and looking surprised by her sister's position. I asked her, "Were you really surprised?"

"No. I guess I shouldn't be. She's been like this her whole life. Her needs have always been more important and she's accused me of not spending enough time with our parents a million times." I asked her to try three things when she talked with her sister again: first, to expect that Laura would be critical and self-focused; second, to apologize for hanging up; and third, to reflect back her argument for why the party had to happen on the dates Laura chose. To help her get the reflective listening right the first time, I told her to pretend she was a television news anchor she worked with, pretend she was conducting an interview, and simply reflect back what was said without reacting to it. This last bit was important. I didn't want her to act angry (if she felt that way), get defensive, or pursue any agenda other than reflecting back what her sister told her. I promised we would get to the issue of when to have the party soon enough. She gave it a try and this is how the conversation went when Carol called Laura on the telephone.

"Hello," Laura answered curtly.

"Hi, it's Carol."

"I know who it is. I saw your number come up. That was rude and uncalled for."

"Look, I hear what you're saying, that was rude and uncalled for," Carol said, reflecting back what she heard without agreeing or apologizing for calling her a bitch and hanging up.

"I'm busy. What do you want?" Laura said impatiently.

"I wanted to see if we could make some progress on the party dates. Can we talk about this for a minute?"

"I've already made some progress," Laura said. "I looked into a hotel for the dates I gave you."

"So you did some research on hotels for the seventh and eighth," Carol simply reflected back, biting her tongue and taking care to not let her irritation show.

"Yes. The seventh is booked everywhere, so it looks like the eighth."

"So the eighth is the best date then," Carol said, sticking to the script.

"Yes, that's right," Laura said, sounding more relaxed.

"Can I ask you a question about the dates you considered?" Carol asked.

"What about it?"

"Can you tell me again why those dates were best?"

"I'm not going to argue about this."

"I don't want to argue. I promise I won't. I just realized I didn't really listen last time. Can you tell me again?"

Sounding impatient, Laura said, "Like I said, the girls' school schedule and dance classes interfere with the week before and after. I'm just too stressed to do it any earlier, and afterward we're going on vacation. These are the best dates."

Best dates for you! Carol thought but didn't say. Focusing on making sure she understood Laura, Carol said, "Just so I understand, the girls' school and dance schedules are keeping you and them really busy, and then you have to get ready for vacation the week after the eighth. Right?"

"Yes. That's right," Laura confirmed.

"It sounds like you're really stressed out with how busy a time that's going to be," Carol said, feeling proud of herself for not succumbing to her anger and focusing instead on the simple task of listening and ensuring she understood correctly by asking questions and reflecting.

"It really is stressful. And you'd think I could get more help from their father but he's stressed too with that new contract."

"Honestly, I don't know how you two juggle it all," Carol said, actually feeling a little empathy.

"I don't know either. Sometimes I want to pull my hair out."

"I would feel the same way if I were you," Carol said kindly, but confessed to herself that she would pull her hair out if she were Laura no matter what the situation!

"So, how are you?" Laura asked.

Carol couldn't tell me many details about what happened next, because at the time she was in shock. According to Carol, her sister "never" asked her how she was doing. Laura thought Carol had it easy. Feeling tentative, Carol told Laura about working the last twelve days straight with no time off and how she had two deadlines the week of the seventh. She explained that things would not slow down for her until a month after their parents' party. Laura didn't say much other than to comment that Carol shouldn't work for slave drivers. They talked for a minute longer and then hung up without revisiting the party.

Later that day, Laura called Carol and said, "I was thinking, maybe we should throw the party later this summer after we get back from Maine. Things are just too hectic for me right now." As it turns out, this was the time Carol had said her work slowed down in their earlier conversation. But Laura made no mention of that being the reason for her proposal. Laura didn't say, for example, "I was thinking we should do this during a time that works for you," which is what Carol *wanted*, but instead proposed a time that worked for Carol, which is what she actually *needed*.

At no time during these two conversations did Carol get sidetracked by the "I'm right, you're wrong" arguments they had had many times before (whether Carol cared enough about the family; whether she had it easy compared to Laura; or whether Laura was selfish and should consider Carol more).

Carol told me, "In a small way, I felt closer to her," and said she was surprised by the feeling. I wasn't surprised, because whenever two people really listen to one another and appreciate the other person's experience, there's a connection. And although Laura didn't appreciate her younger sister's experience explicitly by saying something like, "Let's see if we can find a date that works for you, too," she changed the date to a time she knew worked for Carol. By her actions she showed she not only listened, but apparently cared—whether she knew it consciously or not.

How to Not Sound Fake

Whether I am teaching reflective listening to siblings, couples, business partners, lawyers, managers, doctors, or parents of difficult teens, I always hear something along the lines of, "But I am not a journalist. It sounds fake. Artificial. It will never fly with my [fill in the blank]." If you are thinking the same thing, I agree with the first part but not with the "it will never fly" part. When you're doing reflective listening, I want you to *think* like a journalist, not become one! When a journalist conducts an interview he or she is not negotiating an impasse. You, on the other hand, are.

And I'm not going to tell you that when you first try this, you might not encounter some resistance, which is what Thomas found when he was trying to persuade his colleague to see things his way. Thomas is a partner in a large New York City law firm who had reached an impasse with Charles, a more senior partner. For several weeks they had been arguing about the budget for their pro bono unit. Most law firms do some pro bono work, but this firm had an entire team dedicated to this endeavor and a long-standing reputation in the community for doing that work.

In essence, this was the underlying disagreement: Thomas wanted a substantial increase in the annual budget for the pro bono unit and felt the added investment would be worth every penny in terms of the firm's image and ability to attract new business. He also felt it was the right thing to do—to give back to those who were less fortunate. But he needed Charles's vote at the annual budget meeting, and, to put it bluntly, Charles thought Thomas's idea was "nuts."

As Thomas reported it to me, their conversation went something like this:

CHARLES: This is nuts. We can't afford that kind of increase! I can't vote with you on this.

THOMAS: Are you kidding? We can afford this and much more.

CHARLES: Out of whose pocket? Mine? Yours?

THOMAS: Don't worry, I'm not proposing that we dip into your bonus.

CHARLES: I support our pro bono work as much as you do.

THOMAS: Then support this.

CHARLES: I can't.

By the time I met him at one of my seminars, Thomas had tried several times to convince Charles of his point of view, always with similar results. As we considered the impasse together, I asked him to describe the temperature of their discussions. Usually, he said, they became hot almost immediately. I asked Thomas to do what psychologists call a "reverse role-play" with me—I would play Thomas and he would play the person he was arguing with, in this case Charles. Reverse role-play is a valuable tool that helps people to better understand the impact they have on others. Taking our respective roles, Thomas and I reenacted the argument you read above. After the role-play I asked, "Tell me how you—as Charles—felt when Thomas told you not to worry because he was not going to dip into your bonus?"

"Criticized. You were being sarcastic and calling me Ebenezer Scrooge."

"And what was the emotion associated with that thought?"

"Anger. I was pissed and defensive."

> Reverse role-play is a valuable tool that helps people to better understand the impact they have on others.

After he realized that his response had made Charles defensive, I suggested that Thomas use reflective listening to disarm his partner. But he resisted, saying it would sound awkward and unnatural and that Charles would "see right through" him if he tried it. What he meant, however, was that he could not reflect back Charles's accusation that his proposal was nuts. "I can't sound like I agree with that!" he said. "He'll know I'm up to something."

I explained that he was, indeed, up to something, but that it was neither manipulative nor Machiavellian, and if he had to explain what he was doing, he could.

We practiced several times until Thomas felt confident enough to give it a try. I asked him to call me after the budget meeting to tell me how it went. When I got that call, Thomas was elated. "I got his vote!" he exclaimed, as if he could not quite believe it himself.

After congratulating Thomas, I asked if Charles had accused him of being up to something. He said, "As predicted. I asked him out to lunch and brought up the topic again in the way you suggested. This time, he actually used the word 'insane'!" Thomas said, laughing. "And, of course, he reiterated his position that the firm could not afford it. So I said, without being sarcastic, 'Let me be clear about this. My proposal sounds a bit insane. It's poor judgment on my part. Right?' Then he said, 'Well, I didn't accuse you of drinking on the job or anything, but yes, it most certainly is poor judgment.' But I stayed the course and said, 'Just so I'm crystal clear, we can't afford this kind of expenditure. Right?' Then, just as I thought he would, he gave it to me: 'You're agreeing with everything I'm saying. I don't believe you!' "

Charles thought that because Thomas was not immediately contradicting him—or making an effort to clearly distinguish his view from his partner's by saying something like, "Just so I'm crystal clear, *your view* is that we can't afford this . . ."—he was actually agreeing. And because he didn't believe that Thomas had actually changed his mind about this issue, he was suspicious.

Thomas, however, had been practicing, and he responded as I had suggested. "Yes, I am repeating it back because I didn't listen to your position on this before. I just dismissed it. I don't want to talk about my opinion right now. I want to understand yours and the reasons for it. If I can ask you some more about this, I won't bring it up again after today. You game?"

And he was. By not evading the question, by immediately admitting that he was, indeed, doing something different by reflecting back what Charles had said—even the uncomfortable part regarding his sanity— Thomas was being transparent. I will tell you later how he got Charles to help him. For now, the main point I want you to take from this is that LEAP is not about being sneaky and manipulative. If someone accuses you of that, you can say you were reading a book on negotiations, or arguments, and realized you had not been listening, so you decided to try something new. By acknowledging you had failed to do something in the past and are now trying to do something different to correct that failure—like Thomas did at lunch—you are asking for the other person's help. You are creating a new connection where previously there was a disconnection. You are being open and honest about why you're doing what you're doing, and nine times out of ten you will then be able to proceed with more reflective listening.

Of course the example given here is a business situation, which many people may find easier to negotiate since it's not unheard of to follow a script of one kind or another in certain situations. That's why, in my experience, using reflective listening in a personal situation more often leads to the accusation that you sound like a therapist or sound fake. But the solution is the same. Like Thomas, you should say:

- you're right, I am repeating what you said;
- it's because I didn't listen to you before;
- I'm trying to make sure I understand you this time.

Be direct and honest. Admit that you are repeating, or reflecting back, what your loved one said because you feel you didn't really listen and respect what he had to say last time. You don't want to make the same mistake twice. You're indeed doing something very different.

Listening to the Hard Stuff

When someone is on the attack, it's hard to stick to reflective listening. You will want to take the bait and defend yourself or mount a counterattack. We've already discussed why you don't want to do that, so I won't waste our time going over it again. And I won't talk about how to lower your own temperature since we have covered that as well. But we do need to talk about how a defensive and critical adversary can lure you into making some common mistakes. If you are aware of them, they will be very easy to avoid. Let's look at some examples.

Teenagers can be among the most difficult people to listen to. The irony is that we were all there at one time, yet when we hear their complaints and accusations—that we're stupid, unfair, or mean—we begin to wonder if an alien being has possessed our once respectful and grateful child. That's what happened when Roberta was trying to use LEAP with her fourteen-year-old daughter, Amanda.

Roberta told me that whenever she tried to use reflective listening with Amanda, her daughter just seemed to become angrier and more obstinate. I asked her to tell me about Amanda so I could take her part as we role-played their arguments and tried to figure out what, if anything, Roberta might have been doing wrong. "Amanda is fourteen going on thirty," she began. "She's very smart and mature in many ways, except when it comes to dealing with her mother. She hates me! Everything I do is wrong, and according to Amanda all I want is to control her. It's exhausting just trying to get her to go to bed on time."

"Stop right there. Let's start with that issue," I said

"Well, on school nights I want her in bed by eleven. She turns the lights out at eleven but she stays up sending messages to her friends on her cell phone. I found out when I got the phone bill and saw that one night she was up until almost three in the morning!"

"What did you say?"

"I didn't *say* anything. I bawled her out good! She lost her phone for a week."

"Was that reflective listening?" I asked, smiling.

"God, no!" she said with a laugh. "I'm not that dense! I get the idea. I was just too angry to try reflective listening then."

"Okay. Have you tried it since then?"

"Yes."

"Has it helped?"

"No. Earlier this week I caught her messaging her friends on her computer past midnight. It seems that we're still stuck."

The Three Es

Roberta wasn't dense, but I suspected she was making some of the common mistakes most people make when trying to use reflective listening during an especially hot conversation. They were engaged in a toxic argument, and the three Es were out in full force:

- Entropy
- Escalation
- Evasion

Entropy is when previous arguments have sapped all the energy out of new attempts to resolve the impasse. In this case, it resulted in Roberta and her daughter having little motivation to revisit the topic. Escalation—an increase in the intensity of the arguments—was pretty easy to spot, because the last couple of times the mother and daughter tried to address the situation, they both ended up yelling, name-calling, and worse. Now they had reached that point of the impasse where evasion took over, and Amanda was passive-aggressively doing sneaky end runs around her mother by using her computer instead of her cell phone to message her friends.

The price they were paying was enormous. This mother and daughter had always been extremely close. Roberta used to trust Amanda but now found herself wondering what else her daughter might be doing when her back was turned.

I wanted to identify what Roberta was doing wrong when she thought she was using reflective listening. I asked her to role-play what had happened. Roberta played herself and I played Amanda.

"Why is it *so* important for you to stay up past your bedtime?" Roberta asked.

"It just is. All my friends stay up later than me. It's the only time we can talk. It's stupid and embarrassing to have an eleven o'clock bedtime," I said, imagining what Amanda might say.

"You feel that past eleven o'clock at night is the only time you can talk with your friends. Is that right? Maybe if I helped you more with your homework you would have time before bedtime to do that," Roberta responded.

"That's not what I said! You're not listening!" I shouted.

"That's exactly what Amanda said!" Roberta gasped, breaking out of our role-play. I was not as surprised as Roberta that I had intuited her daughter's reaction. For one thing, it's easier for someone outside the situation to really listen to both sides of the story. For another, Roberta had made all three of the mistakes people most commonly make when they're learning how to use reflective listening. I could have predicted Amanda's reaction based on that alone.

Common Mistakes of Reflective Listening
- Omitting
- Contradicting
- Reacting

Omitting

When reflecting back what they've heard, most people unconsciously omit those things they feel they can't or won't agree with. What did Roberta omit? Go back and look at what "Amanda" said and then at Roberta's attempt at reflecting it back. Can you see what she left out?

She left out the one thing that seemed to be most important to Amanda, which was that her bedtime was "stupid" and she felt "embarrassed" by it.

"Why didn't you reflect that part back to her?" I asked Roberta.

"Because it's *not* stupid and it's ridiculous that she's embarrassed by it. Besides, it was disrespectful."

"How was it disrespectful?"

"Well, you—I mean Amanda—didn't say I was stupid, just her bedtime was . . . so no, I guess she wasn't saying I was stupid, but it felt that way."

"Of course her bedtime is reasonable and not stupid. But the point of our practicing is to help you learn not to argue your position when you're trying to use reflective listening." Roberta saw my point and we practiced again, and this time she was able to reflect back the part she had omitted before.

Contradicting

I then pointed out another, much more subtle but equally common mistake she had made. When reflecting back, Roberta said, "You *feel* that past eleven o'clock at night is the only time you can talk. . . ." In this context, using the word "feel" is a lot like drawing a line in the sand. It's an unconscious way of contradicting someone. It's like saying, "Let's be clear that this is what *you* believe, not me, and probably not anyone else." Other common phrases that are used to subtly say "I don't agree" include "you believe," "your view is," and "you think." So what's the big deal? Why be so anal about not using those phrases? It's not like you're saying, "I know you believe this is the only time you can talk to your friends, but let's be clear that I don't."

Or is it?

Look at Amanda's reaction: "That's not what I said! You're not listening!" From Amanda's perspective—the only perspective that counts when using reflective listening—after eleven was the only time she could communicate with her friends. It was an incontrovertible truth. She didn't think, believe, or feel it. It was an objective *fact*. When arguments get hot, people usually dig in their heels and experience their subjective point of view as fact. They say things like, "Ask anyone and they would agree with me!" They become dogmatic. Whenever you suggest there's room for interpretation, you will elicit a defensive response.

Reacting

Most people react to what was said by reflecting little or nothing back and, instead, defend their already-stated position. On a positive note, Roberta did not defend herself or the bedtime she had imposed, at least not explicitly. But when she said, "Maybe if I helped you more with your homework you would have time [to talk to your friends] before bedtime," she was reacting to what her daughter had said. *Amanda has a problem—she doesn't have time to talk with her friends—so let me see if I can help her to solve it.* It was a considerate response, especially in light of how defensive and hurt Roberta had been feeling. But it elicited yet another angry reaction from her obviously ungrateful daughter. Why? Because Roberta was not listening. She had not gotten it right; instead she had reacted to what Amanda was saying. Amanda's problem was the *stupid and embarrassing eleven o'clock bedtime* not *time management* after school. By focusing on how she was managing her time after school, Roberta was also stating that she was holding firm to her position and blaming Amanda for not having time to talk with her friends at a reasonable hour. She was, in fact, defending her rightness.

AFTER WE DISCUSSED these common mistakes, Roberta was eager to try with Amanda once more. Unfortunately, however, she didn't think Amanda would be willing to discuss the situation with her again. The last time they talked, Amanda had called her a bitch and Roberta had slapped her. She had never slapped her daughter before, and Amanda's look of shocked betrayal and rage was equaled only by the stony silence that followed. So I gave Roberta some tools for reopening the conversation. *How* she got Amanda to talk about the impasse again is not relevant here—it's so common a predicament that I have devoted all of chapter 15 to it. For now, let's see if she was able to avoid the three common mistakes.

After Amanda once again told her mother that her bedtime was stupid and embarrassing, Roberta began by saying, "Let me see if I understand." I like and recommend prefacing and ending what you reflect back with a statement like this one, because it allows you to then use the person's own words without injecting qualifiers like "you believe," "you feel," or "you think." Other phrases I like are "I want to see if I got this right," "Tell me if I am hearing you correctly," "What I heard you say was," and so on. Here is what Roberta said next: "It's stupid to go to bed at eleven o'clock because that's the only time you can talk with your friends. It's embarrassing because none of them has to be in bed that early. Is that right?"

Roberta sounded very surprised (although I wasn't) when she

reported that Amanda had not reacted angrily to these statements and actually seemed relieved by what her mother had said. That's just how quickly reflective listening can disarm people who are angry and defensive. From this position Roberta was able to befriend Amanda by empathizing with her about the "stupid" and "embarrassing" bedtime, saying, "If I were you I would be embarrassed and frustrated, too." Although on the face of it this comment sounded like she might agree with her daughter, she didn't. She was simply focusing on Amanda's experience with the goal of rebuilding her trust and openness. Roberta next identified areas of agreement and highlighted them in her conversation with Amanda. From this common ground they were able to have a conversation about how to move forward together—finding goals they could partner on.

Learn When and How to Use Your Tools

When I teach LEAP I am often asked why I separate the first step, reflective listening, from the second step, empathy. I do that to emphasize the importance of using reflective listening *before* you move on to empathizing with the other person's feelings. Remember that it's not only necessary to have the right tools in your belt but also to know when and how to use them. If you use your tools in the wrong order they won't be as effective, and could actually prevent you from getting the job done properly.

Imagine if Roberta's initial response to Amanda had been, "You sound really frustrated and angry about your bedtime." This may sound as if she were empathizing with her daughter's feelings, but what she might have gotten back is, "I'm not angry!!!" Then what? They could easily have escalated into arguing about whether Amanda was really angry. Empathizing with someone who has not yet felt listened to and respected can often seem condescending.

It's true that sometimes the reaction to premature empathy can be positive, but whether it's positive or negative, empathy is not reflective listening.

Empathy alone diminishes the power of reflective listening because it allows you to omit saying those things that contradict your point of view. For example, when Amanda told her mother that the bedtime was both "stupid and embarrassing," Roberta could easily have focused on the feelings first, but by doing so she would have missed an opportunity to reflect back her daughter's point of view. She might have said, "You sound frustrated about your bedtime." And Amanda may even have agreed with her mother and admitted to this feeling. But by jumping to empathy Roberta would have missed an opportunity to show respect for her daughter's opinion. In fact, when Roberta did use reflective listening, Amanda was immediately less defensive. Undoubtedly this was because she felt her mother was truly listening and understanding her point of view, something she would likely not have felt had Roberta not reflected back the stupidity and embarrassing nature of the earlier bedtime.

What's more, reflective listening, if used correctly, will actually make you more empathetic than you would have been had you not first used this tool, because when you are using it correctly, you are getting a much clearer picture of the other person's perspective. If the person you are arguing with tells you that you "got it right," in that moment you are truly standing in his or her shoes. So it's important that you learn how to use reflective listening before moving on to the kind of empathy I will talk about in the next chapter.

That said, as you become more practiced at both—as the LEAP melody and words become unforgettable—you will find instances when you can and should use reflective listening and empathy at the same time. In certain situations, using two tools at once will get the job done quicker and more efficiently. First, however, you need to become adept at using each one separately.

Why We Don't Do This More Often

Some people are more naturally comfortable than others with using reflective listening. But in the midst of an impasse, almost everyone reverts to the common mistakes I described above. We do that because of our natural fears. We worry:

1. that if we don't take every opportunity to make it clear we do not agree, the other person will think we have changed our mind;
2. that if we use reflective listening we will sound manipulative or artificial;
3. about how this will solve the problem;
4. about not having time for this.

These worries—which become barriers to doing reflective listening— are understandable and natural. For years I had many of them myself. Let me share some of the lessons that have convinced me not to worry about them any longer.

Lessons Learned

By now, because I have already said this several times, you can probably predict at least part of my response to the first worry. Ask yourself again, how many times have you reminded the other person you don't agree with him? Do you think he forgot? Have your frequent reminders done anything to move the two of you past the impasse? Of course not. Now let's look at the alternative. What if the other person does make the mistake of thinking you agree with him? So what? Contrary to what most people think, I believe that is a good thing. Or what if, for a time, he makes the mistake of thinking you have given up ground? You might think that later on, when you have to clarify that you have not changed your mind, he will feel lied to or become angry all over again. That's a reasonable concern, and in chapter 8 I give you tools for making sure that doesn't happen. Specifically, you will learn how to give your opinion in a manner that helps your opponent save face and clarifies that you were never being dishonest. Instead, you will explain that you did not rush to correct the other person's misconceptions about your opinion because you were focused on understanding and respecting theirs. When we get there, I will give you several ways you can restate your position so that you maximize your opponent's openness to your ideas and quickly extinguish any smoldering feelings of betrayal.

As for the second worry, I have learned that reflective listening can, indeed, sometimes sound manipulative or artificial. It's a problem I began to address on page 81, under the heading "How to Not Sound Fake." I have been accused of this from time to time but I have always been able to explain my intentions with uniformly positive results. That is because my intentions—and hopefully yours—are pure. I explain that because I am very interested in listening and getting it right, I may sound a little like a parrot. I sometimes even apologize for the way it sounds. But I never apologize for doing it—for wanting to make sure I understand the person I am speaking with. Most people accept that explanation and lower their defensiveness, because all I am saying is I want to be sure I understand.

> If the LEAP method makes sense to you and if you have some immediate success with it, you will find yourself naturally becoming more curious and caring about your opponent's point of view.

If, in the moment, you are *genuinely* interested in learning more about the other person's thoughts, feelings, and views—if the desire to know more comes from your heart—it will never sound fake. It is what it is—genuine curiosity. If the LEAP method makes sense to you and if you have some immediate success with it, you will find yourself naturally becoming more curious and caring about your opponent's point of view. So I urge you to try it out in a variety of situations until the lesson is learned, because if you *can* become curious and truly care about the other person's perspective, you will never sound disingenuous.

The third worry is most easily calmed through continued experience with LEAP. The more you use it and succeed, the more likely it is that you will use reflective listening without fear. But if you are just starting out, you don't have the benefit of that experience. All you have at this point is my word for it.

Finally, without fail, every time I lead a LEAP workshop, I hear, "This sounds great but who has time to do it?" The answer is, we all do. LEAP is, as I've said, based on motivational interviewing, a methodology that has been extensively studied and shown to be effective without requiring any more time than people normally spend trying to debate or reason with the person they are trying to persuade.

What you are learning is really nothing more than a different way of communicating. It's like learning a different language for arguing. And while it's true that there will be times when reflective listening slows you down for the moment, in the end you will surely make up that lost time. In fact, what I have learned from using and teaching LEAP for many years is that it saves a great deal of time in the end. Compared to what people typically do, it is a much more efficient way of arguing and moving through an impasse.

NOW THAT I have given you the reflective listening tool, practice it and make it your own. Learn how you can use it in your own unique way so it does not sound artificial or stilted. Then visualize yourself using it so it will be easier to remember when you are in the heat of the moment. Personally, when I visualize myself using reflective listening, I see a small cassette-size tape recorder with a bright red L emblazoned on its case hanging from my tool belt. I imagine myself secretly hitting the Record button as my adversary states his position. When he's done, it automatically rewinds and plays back what was recorded. But what makes this tool super-high-tech—Batman-like—is that when it plays back the recording the sound comes out of my mouth and in my own words. Even better, if needed, it automatically sprays aerosol Valium to calm down the person just recorded!

7

Empathize—in Order to Befriend

"If you just learn a single trick, Scout, you'll get along a lot bet-
ter with all kinds of folks. You never really understand a person
until you consider things from his point of view . . . until you
climb inside of his skin and walk around in it."

—Atticus Finch in *To Kill A Mockingbird* by Harper Lee

Strategic Empathy

The second LEAP tool is empathy—*strategic empathy*. That means empathizing with feelings specifically related to the other person's point of view. If your wife is angry because she thinks you are being dense, you empathize with her anger about your stupidity ("I'm sorry, honey, I appreciate how this looks, and I see how this makes you angry"). If your brother is frustrated with what he considers to be your harebrained idea, empathize with his frustration—and leave out the part about the idea being harebrained. The point of strategic empathy is to zero in on those feelings that are usually the most difficult—if not painful—for you to empathize with. Not to be a masochist, but to give voice to those feelings that typically drive a wedge between you and your opponent. By empathizing with those difficult feelings, you remove the wedge and lessen the opportunity for impasse.

A lot of people get hung up on this tool, because they think I'm suggesting they agree with the other person. That's not it at all. What I'm saying is that you need to empathize with the feelings the other person has about his position, even if you think the position itself is just plain wrong—or worse, crazy.

Consider a situation I recently found myself in, when a friend of mine accused me of being overly critical after I commented that it was difficult to talk on the phone with her. Conversations with my friend were often challenging because she tended to get excited about what she was talking about, monologue for long periods of time (even as long as one hour), and give me very few openings to participate. Although I appreciated her exuberance, I felt our conversations were often one-sided, hence the difficulty. The last time we spoke, after a particularly long description of a situation at her job, she asked me why I had become so quiet. I answered the question honestly. She felt insulted, hurt, and angry with me for being "overly critical." Now, as it turns out, I thought she was overly sensitive to criticism, so we were at a bit of an impasse over who was right. We were stuck there until I was able to reflect her point of view back to her and then empathize with her feelings about me. Although I didn't agree that I was being unreasonably critical (actually, I thought I was giving her great feedback she should listen to), I was nonetheless able to empathize with her feelings. "Look, I can see why you would feel hurt and pissed." As I empathized with her emotions, I honestly *agreed* that I would feel the same way if I were her and, therefore, seeing things the ways she did. I believe it was my empathy and subsequent apology for how my feedback made her feel that ultimately led her to ask me, "What is it you want me to do?"

"Well, I should jump in more," I said, reversing the question. "And maybe you could check in with me more often."

She agreed and our conversations became much more of a dialogue instead of the monologue I had nearly resigned myself to.

At this point, I want to make sure we understand one another perfectly, because people often confuse strategic empathy with more general definitions of empathy that can involve agreeing with a point of view or argument or expressing sympathy. This kind of empathy is neither of those things. Rather than feeling sympathy *for* another person, strategic empathy puts you in the other person's shoes so that you are able to feel *with* him or *as one* with him. In fact, the term "empathy" was coined in the early twentieth century to translate the German psychoanalytic term *Einfühlung*, meaning "to feel as one with." And that is exactly what you are trying to accomplish when you use empathy as a tool for breaking an impasse. You want to experience, as closely as possible, the emotions your opponent is feeling.

When you're at an impasse, it may seem there's no room for empathy at all, but, in fact, there are *always* areas in which you can empathize. You may want to express your understanding of those feelings in terms like, "If I were you I would feel very frustrated," "I think anyone would feel angry in your situation," "I can see why you're excited about this proposal," and "If I were in your shoes I would be worried and distrustful as well." But the first step is always to try to actually feel what the other person is feeling. If you can do that, it will lower your own defenses and make you much more persuasive when it comes time to push ahead with what you need.

You need to empathize with the feelings the other person has about their opinions—even if you think the opinions themselves are just plain wrong or even crazy.

Empathy, a Form of Telepathy?

In a way, the empathy I'm describing is a kind of mental telepathy with which you are already familiar but probably don't use nearly as often as you could or should. Think of a movie that made you genuinely happy, scared, or sad. For example, in Frank Capra's holiday classic *It's a Wonderful Life*, did you find yourself smiling, feeling joy, or perhaps even crying when George Bailey stood with his family in front of the Christmas tree, tearfully grinning from ear to ear, his small daughter wrapped up in his arms, as a parade of friends and neighbors filed in to donate money to save Bailey Building and Loan and keep George out of jail? Did you feel some of those feelings now as you recalled that scene? If you did, I would argue that you were using a kind of telepathy. How is it that you could feel the same or similar emotions—actually *feel*, mind you, not simply identify—that George Bailey felt so many decades ago? It's a kind of mental telepathy and time travel when you think about it. If you didn't see this movie (or didn't feel this way when you did see it), take a moment now to think of another character in a film with whom you did empathize—feeling their anger, sadness, fear, or joy.

The success of movies and literature depends upon our ability to see and *feel* ourselves in the characters they portray. By sitting and watching, by not having to interact with the people we meet on film and in the pages of a good book, we are at our most open and, therefore, most able to tap into our natural ability to empathize. My point is that you can and should do this even when you are in the midst of a toxic argument.

> Empathy creates a union of experience that makes it impossible, if only for a moment, to see the other person as an adversary.

When you truly feel what the other person is feeling, it will lower your defenses and make you less threatening, thereby giving you more power to persuade. There's a reason for that: When you convey to another person that you understand and appreciate how he or she feels, it becomes very difficult for that person to continue to think of you as an adversary. If you feel someone is *Einfühlung* with you—you feel as one with the person—you cannot feel, in that moment, that he is against you. Empathy creates a union of experience that makes it impossible, if only for a moment, to see the other person as an adversary.

Sounds good, but how in the world can you empathize when you're angry or simply bewildered by someone else's argument? It's actually very simple.

How to Tap into Your Natural Ability

To tap into this innate ability, you first have to mentally remove yourself from the argument. To do that, I want you to imagine you are sitting in a comfortable chair reading a good book or watching an engrossing film. Now, see your opponent as a character in the story. From that chair, ask yourself, *What are the emotions this person is feeling?* If you are more courageous—and I hope you will be—you can do a reverse role-play like the one you read about earlier. Pretend you are an actor improvising on-stage. Your only direction is to play the part of the person with whom you are at an impasse and say out loud what he or she would say about your disagreement. Think of an impasse you are in and try this now out loud—if you're not alone, close your eyes and do it in your head silently—and see if you don't feel a little of what your opponent is feeling.

To see how this works, let's look at Dan and Rachel, a couple who were arguing about whether to move to Chicago, where Dan had been offered a job. They both had careers and made a good living. If they moved, Dan would make more money, but, more important, the position he'd been offered was the job he'd always dreamed of having.

The sticking point for Rachel was not having to give up her job; it was whether to disrupt the lives of their two school-age children. Rachel didn't want to do that, and the impasse she and Dan had come to was causing frayed nerves and a great deal of hurt on both their parts. Their disagreement had turned toxic. During the course of their many arguments Rachel had accused Dan of being selfish and shortsighted and not caring about the needs of their children. Dan, for his part, had accused Rachel of being selfish and short-sighted as well, and of not sacrificing as much as he had to make their relationship work. These accusations were not so direct and ob-vious, but they were no less damaging to Rachel's ability to break the impasse.

The first crack in Dan's armor came when, instead of going on the counterattack, Rachel began to listen reflectively to what he was saying, even though she didn't agree that he'd sacrificed more than she had.

By listening without judgment she closed the distance between them while continuing to disagree. By reflecting back what he said she conveyed that she could respect his perspective—if only for the moment.

"What you're saying, if I am listening correctly, is that you have sacrificed more for us than I have and you feel it's your turn now. Right?" she asked.

"Don't humor me," Dan said, still feeling defensive.

With no hint of condescension or sarcasm, feeling truly curious, Rachel replied, "I'm not humoring you. I really do want to understand. I hear you saying that you've given up more than I have. That's it, isn't it?"

"Yes. Like I said, when you got your first job I moved for you."

"Wait. I think I get it. Can I tell you what I think you're saying?"

"Fine," Dan answered, still angry and a little suspicious.

"Honest, Dan. I really am listening, and it sounds like you feel you've given more, and you want me to give something back. You feel I am not willing to do that. Is that right?"

"Yes, basically that's right," he said, looking much calmer.

At that point, although she had lowered the temperature of their argument, Rachel didn't believe they were any closer to making the decision they needed to make. They were both still entrenched in their positions of wanting to move and refusing to move. Where Rachel was getting stuck was not being able to use the empathy tool. She just didn't think she could empathize with Dan's feelings. "I don't feel his anger about this and I don't know how to do that because he's not right," she told me.

Although she recognized that her husband was angry, she felt he shouldn't be, and, consequently, she was unable to get inside the anger, much less recognize what was fueling it.

I pointed out that when we are dealing with feelings there is no right or wrong, there is simply what the other person feels. People cannot help what they feel, at least not initially. From where I sat—at a distance that was not unlike watching a movie—it was clear to me that Dan felt hurt. Right or wrong, he was saying things that indicated feelings of sadness. And like many of us—men in particular—it was far easier to express anger than to expose the hurt that lay beneath it.

> When we are dealing with feelings there is no right or wrong. There is simply what the other person feels.

To help her to empathize, I asked Rachel to imagine that Dan was a character in a book telling his story in the first person. All she knew about what was going on was his side of the story. I asked her to role-play Dan as the narrator in the book she imagined she was reading and have her tell what was happening from his point of view, using his voice. Her task was to describe any feelings she, as Dan, actually felt as she told *his* story. Game to play along, Rachel faithfully recounted Dan's point of view in his own words. Then, after a moment's hesitation, she said, "I'm angry because my wife doesn't appreciate me."

"Dan, do you feel angry about anything else?" I asked, wanting her to dig deeper.

"I'm angry that my wife thinks I don't care about our kids' having to change schools, because I do care. I would do anything for those kids. I would die for my children."

As she said this, Rachel's eyes began to fill with tears.

"What's Dan feeling now?" I asked.

"He's—I'm really sad. I'm hurt that she would say that about me. I'm hurt that my wife feels that way about me."

By stepping outside of herself and doing a reverse role-play, Rachel could more easily tap into her empathetic abilities. Even better, experiencing her husband's sadness changed her entire perspective about how to go forward. The first chance she had, she asked Dan if he felt angry, and he, of course, said yes. When she then asked if he felt hurt by her accusation that he cared more for his career than his children's being uprooted, he said he hadn't really thought of it that way, but, yes, he did.

Afterward, Rachel told me their discussion made her feel closer to Dan than she had in weeks. At that point, it was easy for her to say, "I would feel the same way if I were you." She then added that she was sorry she'd said things to make him feel that way and that she truly believed he was a wonderful father. It was that moment of *experienced* and then *expressed* empathy that allowed them to move forward and break their impasse. And, more important, it allowed them to begin to repair the damage their toxic argument had done to their relationship.

In the following chapters you'll be hearing more about how this conversation ultimately led to Dan and Rachel's finding a lot of common ground—areas they could agree upon and use as the basis for finding new options to resolve the impasse. Once she lowered her defensiveness and Dan's, they agreed that Dan's career opportunity and their children's sense of stability were both very important. From that foundation they were able to solve the problem because they both trusted that they each had their shared agenda in mind. For now, however, the main point is that Rachel was able to line up next to Dan only after she had actually felt a little of what he was feeling. Before she listened and then empathized with his experience—his frustration and hurt—they had been face-to-face in a shoving match. Afterward, she was next to him with her arm thrown across his shoulder, saying there was nothing stupid, unreasonable, or hard to understand about his point of view. And she was able to do this even though she still believed Dan was wrong and she was right.

The Language of Emotions

As a psychotherapist—I'm sure you could have predicted this—I sometimes ask people, "How did that make you feel?" And, to my unending surprise, I often hear answers that have nothing to do with emotions. Instead I hear things like, "I felt confused" or "It made me feel more confident" or "misunderstood" or "uncertain" or "vindicated," and so on. The experience of being confused, misunderstood, confident, uncertain, or vindicated is not an emotion. You might think it was the imprecision of my question—the word "feel," after all, can encompass a wide range of experiences—that resulted in such answers, but the follow-up question: "I meant, what *emotion* did you feel?" usually doesn't help them get any closer to the answers I'm looking for. Such exchanges have taught me that many people are not as fluent in the language of emotions as they, and I, would have thought. Emotions include, but are not limited to: fear, anger, sadness, joy, and disgust. Each of these also has close cousins, including anxiety, paranoia, frustration, hurt, depression, contentment, and so on.

It is important to know the difference between emotions and thoughts, because emotions influence our thinking and behavior. Emotions are so influential that modern cognitive scientists argue that they are essential to rational thinking, not simply inseparable. Even Mr. Spock, from the television series *Star Trek*, could not escape his emotions, despite being born and raised among a race of emotionless, purely logical beings. In short, the Vulcans (Spock's people) and Descartes had it wrong. You cannot separate thoughts from emotions. And, importantly, each one can change the other.

What you think can change what you feel, and what you feel can change what you think. Your thoughts, perceptions, judgments, and behaviors change, subtly or significantly, depending on the emotions you are feeling. I could cite a great deal of science on this subject, but others, including Daniel Goleman in *Emotional Intelligence*, have written about it in far greater detail than I can here.

> What you think can change what you feel, and what you feel can change what you think.

In any case, I don't think you need to know the science to agree with this proposition because it's also intuitive, isn't it? If you're feeling paranoid or angry with someone, how likely is it that you will think the other person is trustworthy or reasonable? Every utterance will be filtered through your feelings, distorting even innocent and supportive questions, such as "So are you still feeling overwhelmed with work?" into sarcastic accusations that you are a wimp and complain too much.

Here's another example. Recently, I was driving along in my car when another car suddenly and dangerously pulled out in front of me. I was startled and hit the brakes, punched the horn, and heard my tires screech, all at once. In that moment I was startled, scared, and angry.

My amygdala and sympathetic nervous system were fired up. What happened next is interesting. I became angrier because this man who had cut me off—I was certain, for some reason, that the driver was male—then proceeded to drive ten miles per hour under the speed limit. I was convinced he had purposely slowed down to punish me for blowing my horn. My perception, beliefs, and judgment were all changed by my emotions. The first chance I had, I passed this jerk (you probably know where this is headed) and saw that "he" was, in reality, a tiny, frail-looking woman well over eighty years old, hunched behind a steering wheel that seemed to tower over her head. She wasn't some hotheaded young punk; this was a frail elderly woman who was driving slowly because her reflexes weren't what they used to be. She wasn't trying to antagonize me by driving slowly; she was trying to protect me.

Knowing what your opponent is feeling, then, is key to understanding how he perceives you and your position, whether he is likely to respond positively to you, and whether you have gained sufficient trust to move forward to resolve the impasse. Becoming adept at recognizing emotions in others so that you'll have a better idea of what they're thinking is the first reason you need to learn to use the empathy tool. The other reason is to befriend.

Why Empathy Turns Adversaries into Friends

At the police academy, cadets are trained to "command and control" when trying to take someone into custody. After graduation, this training usually pays off. But not always. When they're in a hostage situation and unable to take immediate control, or when they're dealing with an emotionally disturbed person who may be too paranoid to listen to, much less obey, their commands, that training usually backfires. That is why many police departments have specially trained officers who deal with hostage negotiations and people who are emotionally disturbed. These officers need different tools—ones that are not provided at the academy—in their tool belt. I was teaching LEAP to a group of such police officers recently when one, whom I'll call Sergeant Scott, told me about an encounter he'd had with a woman who was clearly emotionally disturbed.

"When we arrived she was backed up against the front door of her house, unarmed but screaming at the top of her lungs for everyone to 'Get the fuck back!' The first two units to respond were standing down and waiting for our team. Her husband had locked her out and then called 911 because she had been screaming and banging on their door. He said she was bipolar and he didn't want her near their children until she was back on her lithium, so he locked the door and told her to go to the hospital. The first officers to respond tried to talk to her, but she went ballistic when they told her she needed to calm down, so they called us in."

Sergeant Scott then described how he had approached the woman with his hands out, palms up, softly repeating the question, "What's the matter, ma'am?" over and over again. She told him he was what was the matter and to "back the fuck up" or she was going to have all their jobs. Sergeant Scott immediately stopped and took one step back, saying, "I'm sorry. I just want to see if I can help you."

"You-can-make-that-son-of-a-whore-open-the-door," she said, running all the words together.

"Maybe I can, but I need to know what's going on first. Can you tell me?"

"He says I'm sick and the son-of-a-whore locked me out. He's the one who's mental," she said, adding, as if it were one long word, "Lockedmeout*lock*himup!" Then she laughed in a high-pitched, yelping way that made Sergeant Scott think her husband's account of her illness sounded about right.

Reflecting back what she had just said, he asked, "So he says you're mentally ill and he locked you out? And you would like us to arrest him? Is that right?"

"Yeah, that's right. What are you going to do about it, Deputy Fife!"

At this point in the story Sergeant Scott told the others in the seminar that, "She was so furious and insulting. All she wanted was for us to break the door down and get her inside. She really wasn't listening to me until I empathized. I stepped back and thought about it. What if this were happening to me? I've got two kids. What if my wife locked me out and told me I was crazy? I would be furious and feel insulted. So I asked her if that's how she felt and she said, 'Damn right I'm furious.' And I said, 'I'd be furious too if I couldn't get to my kids and someone told me I was mentally ill. I'd be taking names.' And suddenly it was gone. The rage was gone, and her demeanor softened as she said, 'I can talk to this one. He's the only sane one in the group!' and she let me approach her."

What diffused her anger so quickly was Sergeant Scott's strategic empathy. He literally felt her anger and humiliation, and whether he knew it or not, that changed his body language and tone of voice. And then he expressed his empathy. All this happened in a matter of seconds. Nevertheless, it was impossible for this woman, in that moment, to see him as anything but an ally. From her perspective he quickly went from being one of them to being one of us, because, whatever other differences they might have had, they felt the same way about her predicament.

WHEN YOU CONVEY empathy it changes how your adversary feels about you and how you feel about him. It is a moment of pure connection that leaves you both unable to see each other as adversaries. It doesn't solve everything and empathy alone will not get you past the impasse to what you need, but it is an important tool you will want to use at every opportunity. The more moments you and your adversary feel such connections, the less defensive and more open you will both be to finding solutions. Moreover, if you are strategic in your empathy in the way I have been talking about, the person you are empathizing with will feel you can relate to his negative feelings about you. He will feel he doesn't have to defend himself and that you genuinely respect him.

8

Now What?

The important thing is not to stop questioning.

—Albert Einstein

Once you listen reflectively and empathize with the other person's feelings, he will begin to ask *you* questions, like, "So then you agree with me, right?" or the flip side of that coin, "Why are you acting like you agree with me when I know you don't?" This may not happen immediately, but once he realizes you have stopped contradicting him and that you know and respect how he feels, his defenses will go down and he will get curious about where you now stand.

So then what do you do?

Use the Delaying Tool

Your instinct, of course, will be to answer the question. And why not, since you know you're right and the other person is, after all, asking. What you should do, however, is delay answering for as long as you can. The purpose of this delaying tool—delaying tactic, some might say—is to keep yourself from blurting out your point of view the first time you're asked, and if you become adept at using it, getting your opponent to ask for your opinion several times before you give it.

Here's how Rachel, who was arguing with her husband, Dan, about whether to move to Chicago, used the delaying tool when, after she'd listened and empathized with him, Dan asked, "So then you agree that I've given up more?" Rachel didn't agree, but she didn't want to say so at that moment. She'd just lowered the temperature on their conflict and didn't want to disappoint and/or anger Dan all over again by telling him she still thought he was wrong. Rachel knew he'd be likely to ask, and she was ready for it. "I promise I *will* tell you what I think," she said, "but right now I feel I am finally starting to understand where you're coming from, and I want to hear some more before I do that. Is that okay?"

"I really want to know."

"Dan, believe it or not, what *you* think about this is more important than what I think. And you're giving me some food for thought. Let me just ask a couple more questions, okay?"

Not surprisingly, Dan agreed; after all, it seemed that she was finally interested in hearing what he had to say. And Rachel, by expressing her sincere interest in his point of view, had successfully avoided telling him she still thought he was wrong—at least for the time being.

Avoiding the temptation to immediately let the other person know what you truly think is going to be difficult at first, but if you remember that this has never worked in the past, it will be a lot easier.

Why You Should Delay

The longer you're able to delay, the more likely it is that the person you're in conflict with is going to listen when you finally give your opinion. For one thing, the longer you are able to listen and empathize with him without disagreeing, the more time he'll have had to experience you as a friend—or at least as someone who is not trying to strong-arm him—and the less likely he'll be to get mad again when you do let him know you still don't agree. In addition, the more you delay, the more he will feel his opinion is being respected and honored, and, as we've already discussed, the more respected a person feels, the more open, honest, and giving he is likely to be. In fact, by the time you've reached this point in the conversation, your "adversary" is already so certain of your respect for his opinion that he's come to believe you might actually agree with him. You want to cement that bond as much as possible before you risk breaking it again.

There's a second reason to delay. Psychological studies have shown that the harder a person has had to work for something, the more he will value it. In one experiment, for example, women were asked to go through either a severe or a mild initiation process to join a particular group. Although they were both joining the same group, those whose initiation was mild judged the group to be dull and boring while those whose initiation was severe evaluated it more positively. The group, in other words, had more value for those who worked harder to get into it. In psychological terms, this is called the effort-justification paradigm. And so, the more a person has to work to get your opinion, the more he will value it when it's given—even if he still thinks you're wrong.

Feeling in Control and Taking Responsibility

But wait!—at the risk of sounding like an infomercial promising six-pack abs in as many weeks—there's more! One final reason to delay giving your opinion has to do with what psychologists call locus of control. The more a person feels in control (has what we call an internal rather than an external locus of control), the calmer, more patient, and even happier he will be. Where a person places responsibility, choice, and control for events in his life can either be with himself (internal locus of control) or with people and circumstances external to him. The experience is usually unconscious but has powerful effects on a person's motivation and experience of responsibility—taking credit or placing blame. Let me give you an example. I travel a lot for my work, and recently I've recognized that when I do, my mood tends to plummet. On one of these trips I was waiting in line to go through security. The man in back of me kept bumping me with his suitcase, and each time I tried to get out of his way, he bumped me again. I was furious!

Without even turning around I began to have all kinds of negative opinions of this guy—that he was inconsiderate, disrespectful, and so on. Then, after I got through the metal detector I was asked to take off my shoes. I've been asked to do that more times than I can count, but this time it just irritated me even more. Finally, the security check was complete and I decided to get a cup of coffee. There was another long line, and by now whatever patience I'd had left was completely used up. I was annoyed with everyone and everything.

The point here is that when you travel by plane, from the moment you enter the airport you have absolutely no control. The only situation I can think of in which you have less control is when you're undergoing surgery. The very act of standing in a line is giving up control to another person or entity. And the impact this loss (or external locus) of control often has on my mood is that I become irritable, I'm easily angered, I'm quick to judge, and, in general, I turn into a curmudgeon.

Now compare this to the way I felt the first time I ever got on a plane. I was in college and I'd saved up my own money to buy my ticket. When I got on that plane, I felt very much in control. I'd done it myself. I'd accomplished something. I had an internal locus of control so I took credit for the experience and had only myself to blame for those aspects that were uncomfortable. The actual situation was exactly the same as the one that got me so angry (maybe a little less security hassle—okay, a lot!), but my perception of it, and feelings about it, were totally different. And with an internal locus of control, my motivation to get through that line was very high.

Even now, when I get on a plane to go on vacation my mood is different from when I'm traveling for business. In fact, that's absurd, because the decision to go somewhere to earn money is as much mine as the decision to go on vacation. It's just that my perceptions and feelings about it—my locus of control—-are different.

It's a principle of cognitive psychology that when a person is depressed, the therapist tries to determine whether the patient feels he has no control and is being pushed around by the world, and then helps him to see the ways he *is* in control so that he can recapture what that feels like. This is exactly the same as what we do when we try to shift the mind-set of the person we're arguing with so he has the experience of feeling more in control. One way we do that is by allowing him to *ask* for our opinion rather than foisting it upon him whether he wants to hear it or not.

Why Delaying Works

To sum up, there are three reasons why holding on to your opinion works to make your adversary less defensive and more open to your views, and why it gives your opinion more weight. By having to ask you for your opinion more than once, the person you are at an impasse with will feel:

1. more respected and obliged to return the favor;
2. that your opinion matters more than it did at first;
3. more in control and responsible for the experience of hearing your position.

Now let's look at how these three psychological truths work in practice. When I give seminars, one of the questions I always ask is how many of the women in the room have been pregnant, and if they were offered completely unsolicited advice by total strangers on the street. The hands immediately fly up, accompanied by laughter. And when I then ask why they're laughing and how they felt about the advice, the answer is almost always that they felt it was intrusive; they felt annoyed, patronized, and, what's more, said they invariably ignored what they were told, however well-meaning or valid the advice might have been. And yet, these same women also admit they've had at least one friend or relative whose advice they've asked for and to whom they've listened. What's the difference? Their chosen *confidant*—think about that word—was someone they trusted and also someone whose opinion they solicited. By asking, rather than having the advice thrust upon them, they had an internal locus of control.

And even when they didn't really like what they were told, even when the advice felt slightly critical, they were not angered by it because they had requested it.

Or, to give another example, think about the difference between your requesting a service and being offered one you haven't asked for. Let's say you call your television cable company to add a premium channel to those you're already receiving. A good customer service rep might suggest there's a way for you to receive two additional channels instead of just one for only a minimal additional charge. If he were really good at his job, he would first ask if you wanted to hear the offer: "Can I tell you about a special offer we're running?" And even if you were not at all inclined to subscribe to additional channels, you'd probably be willing to hear him out because you'd initiated the call and he'd asked you first if he could tell you. In that scenario you would have an internal locus of control. But if the same rep phoned you unsolicited to offer you this "great opportunity" you'd never asked for, you'd be more than likely to get annoyed and hang up. In fact, you probably receive numerous unsolicited "offers" every day that you either delete from your e-mail or tear up and throw out without ever reading them.

It's a matter of whether the other person thinks you're forcing your opinion on him or believes that he's *caused* you to give it by asking over and over again. If he thinks he made you tell him, he's more likely to accept your opinion than he would be if he felt you were shoving it down his throat. Think about it: If I were to ask you over and over whether you agreed with me, and you didn't seem eager to tell me, I'd have no one to blame but myself when I finally coerced you into giving in to my repeated requests.

So, in terms of learning to LEAP, you won't always use the delaying tool—sometimes it won't make sense—but when you can use it, the longer you are able to delay giving your opinion, the more the other person will have experienced you as respecting his and, therefore, the more obligated he will feel to respect yours (or at least hear you out). Also, the harder he has to work for it, the more it will matter when you finally do give it. And if he has to solicit your opinion, the more in control he will feel and, therefore, the less defensive he will be when he hears it. For these three reasons, your opinion will have more weight.

How to Use the Delaying Tool

The delaying tactic needs to be used properly if it is to do its job. Use it wrong, and you could just make things worse. If the person with whom you're in a disagreement sees your delay as evasive or manipulative, the situation will only deteriorate. If you try to delay when your opponent is hell-bent to hear what you *really* think, delaying may make him angrier. And if your attempts at delaying are controlling—if you unilaterally announce you are not going to answer the question— you will get the exact opposite result you want. So if, for example, Rachel had said, "I'm not going to answer that," Dan would likely feel less in control and more angry. Or, if she had *only* said, "I want to hear more," Dan might well have felt that she was just refusing his request and being evasive. Or he might have accused her of sounding like a therapist. To use the delaying tool correctly, you first have to remind yourself that you can't strong-arm the other person; you need to show your respect and give him some sense of control. In order to do that you must first honor the question, which is exactly what Rachel did when she said, "I promise I *will* tell you what I think." Simply by saying that, she was giving Dan control—his question would be answered—which meant that when she asked to hear more, he was much more likely to feel he was *choosing* to tell her. Only after she'd shifted his perceived locus of control did she go on to divert him, at least for a while, from insisting that she give her opinion.

> If you honor the other person's question, he will wait for your opinion.

You may have noticed that it took Rachel a couple of tries before Dan agreed to tell her more about what he thought before she answered his question. When you're trying to delay, you need to think of yourself as a scientist conducting an experiment. If one thing doesn't work, try something else. The more you do it, the easier it will become, and also, the better able you'll be to judge when the temperature of the argument has cooled to the point where the time is ripe for you to answer the question. You'll get a feel for it by really listening to the other person and by paying attention to the impact your words are having on him. If you continue to delay past the point of knowing he is ready to listen, you'll not only be wasting your energy, you'll also risk getting him angry all over again.

The A Tools for Giving Your Opinion

Sometimes, even after you've listened and empathized, the other person won't ask you what you think. This is rare in my experience, and if it happens to you I want you to consider two possibilities. One is that you have not listened and empathized enough and the other is that the person likes talking so much he has forgotten the context of the conversation—that a resolution to the impasse is needed. If it's the latter, you can ask if he or she would be interested in hearing your perspective. You can say something like, "After listening to you, I have a much better picture of your views on this. Can I tell you what I think?" I've never heard of anyone who used the listening and empathy tools receiving a no in answer to this question, and I don't believe you will either.

But whether you have been asked for your opinion repeatedly and delayed giving it or you have had to offer it because the person—despite being cooled down and feeling listened to and respected—doesn't ask, the *way* you deliver your opinion will determine whether it throws more fuel on the fire or continues to douse the flames. If you want to get past the impasse, there are three new tools you now need to add to your tool belt. I often use all three of them together, but sometimes you need only one or two to get the job done. I call these my A tools both to make them easier to remember and because they

are A-list powerful tools you can use whenever you're arguing or negotiating.

Sometimes I think of them as airbags. In other words, they are tools
that help to soften the blow and save lives—or at least relationships.
The three As are *apologize*, *acknowledge*, and *agree*.

Apologize

Apologizing may be the last thing you think you need or want to
do at this point. But apologies can positively transform adversarial
relationships in an instant. A well-placed apology diffuses anger,
puts you at the same level as the other person (or perhaps a step below them), as it communicates humility, and gives your opponent a
way to save face. You may think that if you need to apologize for anything it would be for having delayed so long. But that's not what I'm
suggesting.

Keep in mind the reason you delayed in the first place: because
you're aware that when you do give your opinion it may damage the
trust—the feeling of kinship, at least at the level of feelings—you've
been building. When you finally admit you really still don't agree, the
other person is likely to be disappointed, to feel somehow betrayed,
and to get angry all over again. So what you need to say is that you understand all this, which can be said in a simple apology about how the
opinion you have is frustrating, disappointing, or, in some instances,
hurtful.

Notice that I'm *not* suggesting you apologize for the opinion you're
about to offer, just for the feelings it might engender. You're not saying
I'm sorry I feel this way, but rather *I'm sorry that what I have to say may
make you feel such and such*. What you might say is something like,
"Before I tell you what I think about this, I want to apologize because
what I think might feel disappointing or hurtful." You can even say,
"I'm sorry; I wish I didn't have this opinion because I know you feel so
strongly I am wrong and it frustrates you."

Understanding that difference ought to make the process easier for
you, but if you still feel unable to apologize, you're probably still too
angry, and you need to use the tools I've already given you to shut

down your feeling brain—breathe, escape, and think. Take a few deep breaths, step back, if only for a moment, and think about why you're doing this in the first place—to get what you need.

Avoid the "But" Word

And when you do apologize, just be sure you *don't* use the "but" word, as in, "I apologize if this is going to upset you, *but*, I think . . ." I mentioned this before, but—I mean "and"—I want to emphasize it here again because it is so important. People who are in a disagreement typically stop listening when they hear the word "but." It's as if you had pushed a button on a remote control and shut off their hearing aid. Not only are they incapable of hearing you, but the most likely outcome is that you'll just revert to "butting" heads all over again.

Acknowledge

What is it you need to acknowledge? Certainly not that you still think you're right, although, ultimately, that's more or less what you're going to be saying. Rather, you need to acknowledge that you're not infallible and you might be wrong—even though you clearly don't think so. (And you're *not* going to say *that!*) So after you apologize, say something like, "Also, I could be wrong about this. I don't know everything."

> If you can be flexible, you're more likely to trigger some flexibility in the other person. If you're rigid and dogmatic, you're equally likely to trigger that.

When you do that you are, first of all, indicating that you are flexible. If you can be flexible, you're more likely to trigger some flexibility in the other person. If you're rigid and dogmatic, you're equally likely to trigger that. Remember that LEAP is all about giving in order to get. If you recall my telephone conversation with my mother's nurse, I'm sure you'll see that if I'd admitted I might be wrong about the HIPAA rules (even though I knew I wasn't) instead of insisting I knew them a lot better than she, I'd probably have persuaded her to help me a lot sooner and with a lot less aggravation on both our parts, because I'd have been exhibiting flexibility, and by doing so, inviting her to do the same.

Acknowledging that you could possibly be wrong is also a way to convey respect, because you are not insisting you are wise and the other person is ignorant. It's the same principle Benjamin Franklin wrote about in his autobiography—which is so important I am going to quote part of it a second time—when he said, "I made it a rule to forbear all direct contradiction to the sentiment of others, and all positive assertion of my own. I even forbade myself the use of every word or expression in the language that imported a fix'd opinion." If it worked for Benjamin Franklin, who broke many seemingly insurmountable impasses, it can work for you.

Agree

I've already said you're not going to be agreeing with the other person's opinion. So what is this about? Here you're going to ask her to agree that you disagree. In other words, you'll be indicating that you respect her opinion and hope she'll respect yours: "I hope we can just agree to disagree on this. I respect your point of view and I won't try to talk you out of it. I hope you can respect mine."

Returning once more to that conversation with my mother's nurse, I was never going to convince her she was wrong about the rules or that it was okay for her to break them. If we were ever to get past our impasse, we needed to agree to disagree on those points and move forward from there in a way that would allow her to give me what I needed without either of us having to say we were wrong. In the case of Rachel and Dan, they needed to set aside the question of who had sacrificed more in the past so they could deal with the problem at hand—how to honor Dan's legitimate belief that taking this new job was a career move he couldn't pass up and at the same time honor Rachel's equally legitimate concerns about uprooting the children.

Moving Past Disagreement

Using the three As, when you sense it's the right time to give your opinion, you might say something like, "You know, I haven't wanted to get into my opinion again, but since you keep asking, I'll tell you. But first I want to apologize because I think it will upset you and I want you to know I could be wrong. I just hope we can agree to disagree about this. I think . . ." When you use this method, the person with whom you're arguing will be hearing your same old point of view—the one with which he still disagrees—in an entirely new way. And if you think this takes a lot of time, read my suggested script again out loud. I just did and it took only ten seconds.

To see how this works, let's rejoin Dan and Rachel's conversation.

"So you agree I've given up more?" Dan eventually asked again.

"I didn't want to get into this because, as I said, I think that how you see it is more important than what I think, but I'll answer if you really want to know," Rachel replied.

"Tell me," he said, more as a challenge than a request.

"Well, I'm sorry for what I am going to say, because it isn't what you want to hear. . . ."

"So then you do think you've given more!" Dan said.

"Sweetie, do you want me to tell you or not? I don't particularly want to get into this, but I will if it's important to you."

"All right. I'm sorry I interrupted. You were saying . . . ?"

"That I'm sorry my opinion might make you angry. I'm sorry it's not what you want to hear, and I recognize I could be wrong. I mean, how do you measure something like that? I just know how I feel about it, and I hope we can disagree about this and focus on the things we *can* agree on. I guess I really don't think you gave up more. But please—I promise not to try to convince you I'm right, and I hope you can give me the same."

"What are you saying? That you gave more to this family than I did?" Dan asked.

"No. I didn't say I gave more. How in the world can we ever figure that out anyway? All I'm saying is I don't think you've given more either. If you feel you have, I can give you that. I just hope we can disagree about it and talk about something more fruitful."

"Like what?"

"Like what would be best for the kids. I know you want that as much as I do. And I don't know anymore if staying here would be what's best for them, especially if it's going to drive a wedge between us. Can we talk about that?"

By giving her opinion the way she did, Rachel communicated a great deal of respect for her husband and, more important, for his point of view. Because of that, she and Dan were ultimately able to move past their irreconcilable disagreement and find something on which they could agree—that they both cared deeply about their children and wanted the best for them. Once they'd done that, they needed to work together to figure out what made the most sense for the entire family.

RACHEL AND DAN were equal partners in a marriage, but there are other situations in which the difference of opinion occurs between two people who are not equally powerful. I'll be discussing a variety of those scenarios in part 3 of this book, but to show you the value of using LEAP to sidestep an impasse even when you do have the power to bulldoze your way through it, let's take a look at Brad and Elaine.

Brad, the CEO of a large corporation, had been arguing with his CFO, Elaine, about an external audit that had been requested by his board of directors. Elaine felt the board was questioning her ability to do her job and had, quite understandably, become defensive. She didn't think the audit was necessary and believed the board was simply overreacting to recent events in the news. Brad worked for the board and Elaine worked for Brad. He felt compelled to honor the board's request—though he was not required to do so—and also thought the idea was a good one. But he didn't want to offend Elaine by forcing his decision on her. He much preferred that she herself came to see the value of complying with the board's request. As her boss, he was practicing one of the fundamental principles of effective leadership described in both *Good to Great* by Jim Collins and *The 7 Habits of Highly Effective People* by Stephen Covey. He was placing a high value on the quality of his relationship with his employee. He knew the audit would get done one way or the other, but he didn't want to alienate Elaine in the process.

First, he listened carefully to her explanation of why such an audit would be a waste of precious time and resources and why she felt it could wait until the fourth quarter of the fiscal year, when it was already scheduled. After he had carefully reflected back his understanding of her opinion—without reacting to it or contradicting it in any way—and empathized with her concern about an "early, unneeded audit," Elaine asked the golden question: "So you're seeing my point. Can I assume you're on board with waiting until the fourth quarter?"

Using what he'd learned from me about LEAP, Brad didn't answer at once. Instead, he used the delaying tool a couple of times so Elaine could have more experience of their positive, affirming interactions. He said, for example, "I'll answer that, but I'm getting a much better picture of your arguments and I would like to hear more. Can you give me more reasons?" Elaine continued enumerating her reasons and then asked again what Brad thought. Only when he saw that she was less defensive and able to hear him did he ask, "You wanted to know if I was on board with saying no to the board. Do you still want to know what I think?"

Notice that he allowed Elaine to remain in control, so she could experience an internal locus of control, by asking if she was ready to hear his answer. Brad knew he was going to tell her what he thought, but by getting her to decide when to hear it, he was allowing her to perceive it as her choice. When she said that she did, he used the A tools. "Look," he said, "I'm sorry, because this will disappoint you. I could be wrong. But I want us to respect one another. Let's agree to disagree this time. We have to do the audit now, and I believe I can count on you despite the fact that you think it's a bad idea. Am I right about that?"

"Of course you can," Elaine quickly replied, with a smile that showed her obvious affection for her boss.

At Brad's request I later consulted with his management team and had an opportunity to ask Elaine about the interaction she'd had with her boss. I asked her how it felt when Brad presented his decision the way he did. "I felt like he truly considered my argument," she said. "He respected my advice and maybe even thought I was right. But I suppose he was stuck between a rock and a hard place with the board, and ultimately I am behind him."

Before he learned about LEAP and acquired the tools to apply it, Brad very well might have simply dismissed Elaine's concerns and told her, "This is not a negotiation. I've made my decision," because doing that would have been consistent with his view of himself as a strong leader. But when I later asked if using LEAP had made him feel less strong, he responded emphatically, "Not at all! In fact, I felt stronger. I felt more like a leader somehow. I could see how much Elaine appreciated my questions, my listening, and my telling her my decision in the way I did. I think she liked me more for it, and I think she'll be even more loyal and work harder for me now."

So in the end, by listening, empathizing, and delaying before giving his opinion, Brad turned a situation that had threatened to hurt his relationship with a valued employee into one that caused her to feel even more positively about him.

THE PURPOSE OF the LEAP tools we have covered thus far (listening, empathizing, delaying, and using the three As) is to reduce the temperature of the argument, lower defenses, and transform an adversarial relationship into an alliance. The alliance at this point is founded on the other person having an experience of respect, trust that his arguments will be carefully listened to without argument, and a feeling of kinship with you at the level of emotional experience ("He understands how I feel"). He also feels more in control and, consequently, less like he has to strong-arm you. Now the ground is fertile for finding areas of agreement and ultimately working together, as partners, to cultivate that common ground to yield a solution that addresses your shared interests.

9

Agree—with Your Adversary

Vizzini: INCONCEIVABLE!
Inigo Montoya: You keep using that word. I do not think it
means what you think it means.

The Princess Bride

Now that you've given your opinion, you have highlighted, once again, the disagreement. You've corrected any misconceptions that you have surrendered caused by listening reflectively, empathizing, and being reluctant to inject your point of view. You may wonder if you're now back at square one and it will be impossible to agree on anything substantive. Not at all—because you have transformed the relationship from one between two adversaries to one between friends, or at the least, viable collaborators. Friends and collaborators are much more effective than enemies at finding workable solutions. But before you can find solutions, you will need to discover those areas in which you agree.

By using the term "agree," I'm not asking you to change your opinion or lie about what you really believe. I am also not talking about negotiating: for example, "You want one hundred dollars, I'll come up from fifty and give you seventy-five dollars." What I'm saying is that, even in what appears to be the most black-and-white situation, there is always some common ground, some goal on which you and your new-found friend can agree. Finding that strip of shared turf, however narrow it may be, is key to developing new options. Without new options that go beyond "It's my way or your way," you will never move past your impasse and become partners instead of adversaries.

This is so important I will say it again in a different way. Together you have to stake out common ground—things you agree on—because only by standing together on that ground can you work together to build solutions. It's like nineteenth-century homesteading in the American Midwest. On covered wagons families would race into the prairie to stake out land on which to build their houses, farms, and futures. But without a deed carefully recorded at the land office—an agreement between the homesteader and the government—not a single foundation stone could be laid. Once you have areas of agreement—your deed—you will use them to build a resolution to the disagreement in ways you may not have considered previously. You will still get the house and land you wanted when you started out, but in a brand-new territory.

> Even in what appears to be the most black-and-white situation, there is always some common ground, some goal on which you and your newfound friend can agree.

What, then, can you agree on? On what bit of land, no matter how narrow, can you record your deed? If there's one fundamental thing you and your adversary can always agree on, it's that you're both very unhappy with the way the argument has unfolded. Oftentimes, when we feel we were mistreated, we forget that the person on the other side may feel that way as well. You may also agree that things have improved since you started listening, respecting, and empathizing with your opponent's point of view. Beyond that, however, if you go back and consider what you really *need*, you'll undoubtedly discover there's more to agree on than you might think. In my conversation with the ICU nurse, for example, we both agreed that we cared for my mother—I as a son and she as a nurse. We agreed she had to follow the rules. And we agreed that I, because I had my mother's medical power of attorney, needed to be informed about her case (even though we still disagreed on whether the nurse was "allowed" to fax me her records). Once we were able to agree on those fundamental points—and once both of us were able to understand and accept what it was I really needed—we were also able to find a way out of our impasse. At that point, because she felt listened to and respected by me, the nurse couldn't help liking me at least a little, and wanting to find a way to help me—which she did by reading me the chart she still believed she wasn't allowed to fax me! But what finally opened the door to my getting what I needed was that we agreed.

The Agreement Tool

I see my agreement tool as a parchment scroll rolled up in a leather pouch that's hanging on my tool belt. When I'm ready to use it, I draw it from its pouch and snap it open. At the top of the page I have written "Declaration of Agreement," and beneath that heading are the words "I hold these truths to be self-evident," followed by a list of my beliefs and goals. If I were engaged in a scuffle with a colleague my list might include such statements as "Neither of us wants to burn any bridges," "We both care about getting the job done," "Our impasse has drained time and resources," and "We both want to come out ahead." Depending on the nature of the impasse there may be more specific areas of agreement, such as in the case of my argument with my mentally ill brother. I thought we would both agree that he should have spending money, stay out of the hospital, and be free of the family (and me) trying to convince him he had a problem. Next to each item on the list is a box. I put a checkmark in the box next to each statement with which I believe the other person would agree. Sometimes, to be certain, I have to ask him if what I believe to be an area of agreement is truly a belief or goal we share (Would you agree with me that _____?). Other times our agreement is self-evident (I know we both care about _____).

Another, more dramatic example of how this works was described to me recently when I met the author Pete Earley, who wrote a book entitled *Crazy: A Father's Search Through America's Mental Health Madness*, which was inspired by his experience after his son was diagnosed with a mental illness. As Pete told me, he'd been fixated on getting his son, Mike, to agree that he was mentally ill—something that Mike was not about to do. It wasn't until Pete had given up the need to hear those words that he and Mike were able to find areas in which they *could* agree: Mike didn't want his parents to keep dragging him back to a mental hospital, and his parents certainly didn't want to have to drag him there; Mike wanted to work again, and his parents also thought it would be good if he could find a job; Mike wanted to live with his parents, and they wanted that, too, because when he wasn't with them they were constantly worried about him. Based on these common goals, Mike's parents assured him that they wouldn't take him back to the hospital or make him see a doctor, and that he'd be able to live with them—as long as he refilled his prescriptions and continued to take his medication, which is what they really *needed* him to agree to in the first place. Although they never agreed on the original issue—whether he had a mental illness—the points they did agree on proved key to getting both Mike and his parents what they each needed.

Agreeing Creates a Team

When you're at an impasse with someone, whether you know it or not, the two of you have chosen to be on opposing teams. But once you have disarmed and befriended your adversary, you can start the game fresh and pick new teams. You can turn the situation from "me against you" to "us against them, or it." The way to do that is to agree. Remember Roberta and her daughter, Amanda, who were at an impasse about Amanda's bedtime, and Charles and Thomas, who were arguing about their law firm's pro bono budget? What do you think they agreed on?

Roberta and Amanda agreed they were tired of the tension between them. Roberta asked her daughter, "You must be sick and tired of me riding you about your bedtime."

"Duh?! I *am* sick of it."

"I'm tired too, Amanda, and I wish we were not fighting all the time. Don't you wish that?"

"Yeah, I wish that," Amanda agreed.

They also agreed that Amanda's friends were important to her. Roberta said, "I know you love talking to your friends, and friends are really important. Did you know that I met your aunt Lynndie when we were in high school?" Amanda didn't realize, or had forgotten, that her mother had met her oldest best friend in high school. And to her mother's surprise, Amanda agreed that Roberta should make rules for Amanda. Roberta had asked her, "Do you think it's my job as the mother to make some rules?" Amanda said, "I know it's your job to be the mom. I know you have to make rules." Then she laughed and added, "But they shouldn't be stupid rules!" Roberta laughed with her and didn't take the "I'm right, you're wrong" bait because she was focused on what they *could* agree on—they were tired of fighting, Amanda's staying in touch with her friends was important, and Roberta was supposed to make rules. Voicing these agreements opened the door to a new conversation about how to solve their problem and ultimately led to Amanda respecting the bedtime her mother had given her.

> You can turn the situation from "me against you" to "us against them, or it." The way to do that is to find something—anything—on which to agree.

And what about Thomas and Charles? Once they were able to get past the mutual defensiveness and quick dismissals that characterized their first argument, they were able to have a substantive conversation about the pros and cons of increasing the firm's pro bono budget, and when they did that they found plenty about which they agreed. They agreed that the pro bono work was a moral obligation they shared. They agreed that the work of the pro bono unit had, indeed, brought the firm new business in the past. And finally, they both agreed that

Thomas needed to write a cogent and convincing argument laying out his reasons for believing that the increased budget would pay for itself in terms of public relations and new business. Eventually Thomas and Charles were able to partner on one of their areas of agreement in order to get Thomas the one thing he needed—Charles's vote at the budget meeting.

Let's look at a few more instances in which people with major irreconcilable differences found much to agree on.

RAISE VS. NO RAISE

Cristina wanted a raise because she had reached her five-year anniversary with the company and believed she should be rewarded for reaching this milestone. Peter, her boss, was not convinced. He explained that she had already been given raises at every annual performance review and that what she was asking for was not company policy (although they did give her a framed "five years of service" certificate for her office wall).

Cristina argued that this was not fair; Peter countered by saying it was and that if he gave Cristina an anniversary raise it would set a precedent for every other employee who stayed with the firm for five years, or ten, or fifteen. He was unyielding in his decision. They were at an impasse.

When I spoke with Cristina, I asked her why she had approached her request the way she had. She said she was stressed and needed the extra money, and because a friend of hers had received a raise based on longevity, it made sense to her to ask for a reward based on faithful service. Surprisingly, she knew very little about Peter's view on raises beyond the fact that he reviewed her performance yearly and gave her a raise based on her good review.

After meeting with her boss and listening—really listening—to his views, Cristina understood what motivated him. As it turned out, Peter's philosophy was that if an employee produced more, the company would make more, and he was inclined to share the increased profit with the employee responsible. His was strictly a profit-driven philosophy, while Cristina's strategy had been focused solely on rewarding long-term loyalty. She thought Peter was wrong not to reward such loyalty, but trying to convince him otherwise was not going to get her what she needed.

Once she had listened to him, she was able to empathize with his feelings (that is, his worry about what would happen if he agreed with her first proposal) and found they actually agreed on several points that were key to unlocking the impasse. They both agreed that if she got the raise she was asking for, she could quit the part-time second job she had taken to make ends meet. Without that stress and with more flexibility in her schedule, she would, they were both confident, be more productive. If she did not have to leave every day promptly at five, as she did now, she would be available to help out with end-of-the-day emergencies, and, if necessary, she could come in on Saturdays when there was extra work to be done. By helping him to find his own reasons for doing it—that is, her increased productivity—Cristina convinced Peter to give her the raise she needed, even though she couldn't convince him that he'd been wrong not to reward her loyalty.

SURF VS. STUDY

Dana loved to surf. She was good at it. Not so good that she could compete professionally, but good enough to draw a small crowd of onlookers when the surf was up. During her junior year in high school her mother asked her which colleges she might want to attend. Dana said none. Her plan was to move to Hawaii with her best friend and surf for a year or two. She would get a job as a waitress to support herself.

Their very first discussion of this topic quickly escalated into a toxic argument and impasse. Dana's mother argued that if she didn't go to college immediately after graduating high school, she would never go. Dana said she was sure that one day she would, but not now. Her mother, however, was not reassured, and they remained at an impasse for more than a year. There were frequent skirmishes from time to time as her mother tried to bend Dana to her will, but Dana had made up her mind. There seemed to be no common ground.

After learning to LEAP, Dana's mother backed off trying to strong-arm her daughter into going to college and started to listen and rebuild the trust that had been eroded by their head-butting arguments. She learned that there was, in fact, a lot they agreed on. By putting aside what she thought she wanted—Dana's promise that she would go to college immediately after graduation—she helped Dana to lower her defenses and open up. Mom learned that her daughter had adopted many of the same values about a college degree that she had. Growing up, Dana had listened to her mother's stories and was convinced that a college degree would, in fact, be immensely helpful. She also believed, because her mother's experience was so positive, that college would be "the best time in my life." As they talked more about it, Dana admitted she did want to look at colleges in anticipation of going—but *after* she'd taken her surfing break. The last semester of her senior year, mother and daughter visited four schools together. Mom was ecstatic.

What she really needed, much more than the thing she thought she wanted, was to feel she had done a good job as a mother. Talking to her daughter with the heat turned down on their argument revealed that she had. Their tour of the four campuses lowered her anxiety about Dana's commitment to go to college. Dana was a smart, savvy, and confident young woman. Mom felt she had given her daughter some vital life skills and values and was now confident she would, indeed, go to college. When—not if—she was ready.

FAMILY VS. FAMILY

Mike's father, Frank, refused to come to Mike's wedding. They argued and argued about it, but they were at an impasse. From Mike's perspective his father, a strict Catholic with conservative values, was trying to make him choose between the family he was trying to create and the one he'd been born into. Mike's fiancée, although Catholic, was divorced, and the church had refused to grant her an annulment. Frank said he would not bear witness to marriage vows that were not consecrated in the church. Unfortunately for both men, the first time they tried to talk about it, the common ground they really did share was immediately hidden beneath a thick cloud of toxic smoke.

What happened was that just a few months before the big day Mike heard from his mother that his parents "might not" be coming to the wedding. She refused to explain, and told Mike to speak with his father about it. Incredulous and angry, Mike confronted Frank. "Mom just told me you two might not come to my wedding?!"

"She shouldn't have told you that."

"Why not? Is she wrong?"

"Yes. There is no maybe. We are not going to the wedding. At least I'm not; I can't speak for your mother."

"You're kidding me, right?"

"No, I'm completely serious. For it to be a real marriage you need to do it before God and the church. You need to be married by a priest. You know how I feel about that."

"But we tried and the church won't let us."

"God works in ways we cannot always fathom."

With those words Mike went ballistic. The argument turned hot, and ended with both men raising their voices and Mike calling his father a hypocrite. Worse, he gave Frank an ultimatum: "If you don't come to our wedding, I am never setting foot in your house again."

"You have to do what you have to do," Frank retorted.

"If you're not there, I will never speak to you again!" Mike shouted, upping the ante before turning his back and storming out of the room.

Frank boycotted the wedding, and, despite the best efforts of his mother and siblings to heal the rift, Mike kept his promise. For two years he would go to family functions only if they were held on neutral territory, and even then he refused to say hello to his father. Frank was stoic and claimed he respected Mike's decision.

The impasse continued until Mike and his bride had their first child, a son. Although he'd been putting up a brave front, Frank really missed Mike, and the birth of his first grandson was just the motivation he needed to try and break the impasse. He wrote a letter asking Mike to let him come over and talk. His son relented.

If Frank had gone into their meeting wanting to express his rightness about boycotting the wedding even once, his "peace mission" would have failed. But this time Frank was prepared to listen and learn. He was able to empathize with his son's anger, and when it was his turn to talk, he asked if he could list the things he felt they agreed on. Of course, Mike said yes, which gave Frank the opening he needed to say, "We both agree that this has been bad for the family. This split, if it continues, will be bad for your son, too. You and I can't change the past, but we can control what we do going forward. Agreed?"

"Yes," Mike said.

"You haven't said this, but I wonder if you miss me. I know I miss you. I miss being part of your life."

"I do miss you, but that doesn't make what you did okay."

"I'm sorry about what I did. Truly. And I would be happy to apologize to your wife."

"Then you admit you were wrong?"

Frank bristled but remembered to think about the big picture, what he needed, which was to build a bridge to his son, so he pulled out the delaying tool, because he still believed what he did was morally justified. He said, "We can talk about that later if you insist. For now I would like to focus on what we were just talking about. Would that be all right with you, Mike?"

"I suppose."

"So, we both miss each other. We both feel this has been bad for our family, your wife and mine, and now your son. I would like your forgiveness."

In the end, Mike did forgive his father, despite the fact that Frank never actually said he'd been wrong to boycott the wedding. By using the delaying tactic, Frank was able to avoid what could have been another showdown—in effect, another "I'm right, you're wrong" impasse—and to focus on what was really important, the ongoing relationship between father and son.

Regardless of your own feelings about Frank's decision, he was, in fact, a deeply religious man. Although it tore him up inside, he felt confident he'd done the right thing. To my knowledge, he has never wavered on this. But he never said he was going to boycott the relationship Mike had with his wife, just the wedding. In truth, he did feel great sorrow about what his faith had led him to do. He had prayed about it and looked for a way out of his predicament. His apology was for the pain he had caused. He was truly sorry about that, but he could only deliver the apology effectively after he'd stopped trying to defend himself. At that point, Mike was also able to accept his father's apology because they stood together on common ground.

Common Ground

Just as important as the specific points on which you find you can agree—where you find your common ground—is how you get to that point. By using the LEAP tools, you are respecting the other person's point of view, expressing your own fallibility, and seeking to find a way to resolve the impasse together. By doing all that, you create a strong foundation of trust—shared turf—upon which you can build a partnership. From that point on, you and your adversary will be teammates, and the common ground you are standing on will be your playing field. Now the two of you will have a new opponent—namely, "the problem" as the two of you have defined it together (how to pay for the pro bono work, how to make time to talk with friends, how to justify a raise, and so on). And like a pitcher looking for signs from the catcher, you will decide together what the next pitch should be.

Agreeing When You Do Not Agree

Pop quiz. What are the three A tools? Answer: apologize (for how your opinion may make the person feel), acknowledge you could be wrong (no one, not even you or me, is infallible), and agree (agree to disagree on this one issue).

Remember the second A, acknowledge your fallibility? In addition to using it whenever you give a contrary opinion, you can use it to persuade your new teammate to partner with you to achieve even those goals on which you may not entirely agree. Here's another example from my all-time favorite great persuader, Ben Franklin. The Constitutional Convention of 1787 was at an impasse. The delegates could not agree on the issue of representation, and Franklin is widely credited both by his contemporaries and by historians with providing the key that unlocked the impasse. At the end of their deliberations, Franklin drafted a speech advising compromise. It was read by another delegate because by this time, at the age of eighty-two, Franklin was too frail to read it himself. In the speech, he pleaded with his fellow delegates to "consult, not contend," and observed the following about his own infallibility: "I confess that I do not entirely [agree with all of the provisions of] this Constitution at present; but, sir, I am not sure I shall never [agree with them]; for, having lived long, I have experienced many instances of being obliged, by better information or fuller consideration, to change opinions even on important subjects, which I once thought right, but found to be otherwise." In other words, Franklin said, "I could be wrong," so I am willing to partner with the rest of you even though we do not entirely agree on everything. By saying this he was inviting the delegates to consider their own fallibility and thereby suggest a way in which they could partner with him.

Franklin ended his speech by saying, "On the whole, sir, I cannot help expressing a wish that every member of the convention who may still have objections to it, would, with me, on this occasion, doubt a little of his own infallibility, and, to make manifest our unanimity, put his name to this instrument."

I can only wish the same for you—that if you are finding it difficult to partner with someone because there are still some important areas upon which you disagree, you can, nevertheless, move forward together because, in fact, you do have areas of agreement (if only that you are both fallible). If you can do that, no impasse is too great to overcome.

10

Partner—to Get What You Need

For united we stand, divided we fall

—Tony Hiller and Peter Simons, "United We Stand"

Over the course of my career I've been a team leader in a variety of settings—academic, corporate, government, and nonprofit—and every now and then, when the competition among coworkers hurts productivity and morale, I have to gather the troops to remind them that they're partners, not adversaries. At those times I want to do more than simply state the obvious—that partnering will make them all more productive and happy. I want them to actually experience the difference. So I tell them to pair off and clasp hands across a table in an arm-wrestling position. Then I explain, "The object is to win. Each person gets one point every time the back of his or her partner's hand touches the table. The pair with the highest number of points wins." Most pairs end up with two or three points as they struggle against each other, but there is usually at least one pair that has more than forty points! How could that be? It may have been obvious to you from the start, but if it wasn't, go back and read my instructions very carefully.

Get it now? I said, "The *pair* with the highest number of points wins."

The only way to break an impasse and "win" is to stop thinking of the other person as an adversary. But simply not being an enemy is not the same as being a partner. To make someone your partner, you need to recognize your common goals. That's the purpose of the agreement tool we discussed in the previous chapter. Once you have done that, you will be able to find a way to persuade the other person to partner with you to achieve those goals. Like those pairs of employees who scored more than forty points, you'll stop wrestling with one another and be able to create a game plan that reflects your new relationship as teammates pursuing your shared interests rather than opponents. And that game plan will, more often than not, go beyond the two options you have been arguing about (my way versus yours). But where does that game plan come from?

Getting Past "It's My Way or Yours"

In their book *Getting to Yes*, the authors write about what it takes to succeed at negotiations and identify the vital ingredient as having multiple options to choose from. They argue that many negotiations get stalled because only two options are being considered. I couldn't agree more. But how do you come up with new options? The answer is *you* don't. At least not alone. You do this together *with* the other person. Once you are on the same team, there's room for creativity and new options will occur, because you're no longer wasting your energy and brain power going one-on-one like basketball players, each reacting to the other person's every move. Instead, you are side by side, working toward a common goal.

When you work that way, you are no longer judging the other person's position and finding it wanting. And because nonjudgmental relationships open doors psychologically, more often than not, one or both of you will be able to think more creatively.

Putting Your Heads Together

Once you feel aligned with the other person, it's time to introduce the idea of working together to come up with new options to resolve your impasse. You can introduce those options, you can invite the other person to do so, as I did with the nurse, or the new options might just naturally flow from you both.

Remember Dan and Rachel, who had finally agreed they both loved their children and wanted to do what was best for them? Because Rachel was lowering his defenses with LEAP, Dan was able to concede that uprooting them would be disruptive. And once she had lowered her own defenses, Rachel was also able to tell Dan she agreed it would be a shame for him to pass up such a great opportunity. By mutually acknowledging those areas of agreement, they were able to set aside the fruitless (and not really pertinent) argument they'd been having about who had sacrificed more in the past and seek a solution that would work for the family as a whole.

Dan suggested they try something he had once done during a brainstorming session at work. They sat together at the dinner table after the children had gone to bed and wrote down every idea they could think of. Dan explained it to Rachel this way: "Absolutely any idea that comes into your mind is fair game. We can't censor anything. Also, we can't criticize or judge any of the ideas. Our job is to come up with as many as we can in five minutes and then talk about them."

Although they took the exercise seriously, they both found themselves laughing as they scribbled their proposals. It was fun and somehow funny to them. But the result was as surprising as the experience was enjoyable. They came up with several good options neither of them had previously considered. One by one they took each option from the pile they had made and talked about it, focusing on discovery and highlighting only its advantages. One of the ideas they had both written down, and ultimately found so silly, was that they should divorce. But among the options in that pile was the one they ultimately partnered on: Dan would accept the job and move to Chicago immediately; Rachel and the kids would remain where they were until the school year was over. Dan would come home on weekends and Rachel and the kids would visit him in Chicago on at least two school vacations. Not only would this arrangement keep the family from becoming estranged, it would also allow the kids to gradually become acquainted with their new home. Then, once they were out of school, they and their mother would follow Dan to Chicago. They'd give it a try for a year, and if Dan and the kids were doing well, they'd consider the move permanent. If any of them was unhappy or not doing well, they'd reconsider their options. So, Dan got to have his dream job, Rachel got to cushion the kids as much as possible from the disruption in their lives, and they both knew they had an out because neither was insisting the arrangement had to be permanent.

If you heard only the solution without the process, you might come to the conclusion that Dan and Rachel had bargained. But that's not how it happened. The goal they ultimately partnered on, that got them past the impasse, was one they came up with together based only on a simple idea written on one of their pieces of paper. It read, "Dan moves now, kids finish school year, spend as much time together as possible during that time, then move and decide if permanent." I could tell you who wrote the note, but even that information would be misleading. I don't think the idea sprang from just one of them. I believe it, and its elaboration, came from the synergy of two people putting their heads together in the context of a relationship imbued with trust, respect, and openness.

Jump-starting Partnering

After disarming the other person and finding common ground it can be difficult to move toward working on the problem again, especially at first. And while I don't recommend you follow a script, it might be helpful to see some examples of partnership invitations to get you started: "What would you do if you were in my situation?" "Can we brainstorm together about how to solve our problem?" "If we put our heads together do you think we could come up with another solution that works for us both?"

To go back to another situation we've already discussed, Roberta and her daughter, Amanda, also found some common ground. They agreed they both wanted the tension between them to end, that Amanda's wanting to talk with friends in the evening was normal, and that it was, indeed, Roberta's job to make and enforce the rules in their home. From this common ground they were able to have a conversation about how to move forward. Roberta, once she had listened to her daughter and understood that those evening chats were very important to her, suggested that Amanda finish her homework and stop watching TV by ten p.m. so she could have a full hour to message her friends. She even agreed to remind her a few minutes before ten that it was "time to get on the computer." But she still wasn't certain this would be enough to get Amanda to comply with the new rules, so she asked her daughter, "If you were me, what would you do?" and, to her surprise, Amanda said, "I'd keep my phone charger in your room and turn off the wireless Internet when you go to bed so I wouldn't be tempted." Roberta did exactly what Amanda had suggested. She moved the wireless router and Amanda's cell phone charger into her bedroom. Now, if Amanda wants a charged phone, she has to leave it overnight in her mother's bedroom. And with the router there as well, Roberta is able to turn it off at eleven o'clock. Neither idea had occurred to her until her daughter came up with them.

One night a week Amanda prefers to watch her favorite TV show and text-messages her friends on her phone, but on the other nights she is at her computer, chatting, promptly at ten p.m. Between chats, she showers, brushes her teeth, and gets into her pajamas so she's ready for bed by eleven p.m.

You may wonder why Amanda would have sabotaged herself in this way. But you would be asking the wrong question, because once she and Roberta had settled on their areas of agreement, her goal became helping her mother become more effective at setting boundaries while still being able to message her friends.

By not dismissing Amanda's "chat time" as unimportant or wasteful, Roberta was able to problem-solve with her to incorporate it into the nightly ritual of things that needed to get done. Now, rather than complaining when she hears the "ding" from the computer indicating that Amanda is online, she actually encourages her chats.

And then there were Thomas and Charles. As you learned in the previous chapter, they, too, agreed on many things. They agreed that the pro bono work was a moral obligation and that it had brought both positive publicity and new clients to the firm. After Thomas drafted his memo explaining to the partners how and why the budget increase would bring added value to the firm, he asked Charles to critique it. In the end, although the memo was signed only by Thomas, Charles had made substantial contributions to it. At the subsequent budget meeting he helped argue for the increase and cast his vote with Thomas.

IN THE EVENT you still think, despite all I've told you, that you don't have time for LEAP, let me give you one last example that vividly illustrates how quickly this can work. Remember Sergeant Scott and the woman having a manic episode who had been locked out of her home by her husband? The sergeant got her to calm down by listening to her and empathizing with her predicament. Once she was able to talk calmly, she immediately asked him to help her get into her house. At that point he confessed there was really nothing he could do to force her husband to open the door because, technically, he wasn't breaking the law. They agreed she was at an impasse with her husband and that Sergeant Scott wanted to help her find a way to get back into the house. They also agreed they couldn't stand out on the front lawn all night.

Although he couldn't get her inside immediately, the sergeant thought he had another idea that would help her to get what she needed. Would she be interested in hearing it?

She was.

He explained that if she let the officers take her to the hospital she'd be able to prove to her husband she was sane. She didn't like that idea at first. "I can't trust the doctors, they'll just take his word over mine and lock me up again," she said.

"Well, then, what if I go with you and tell the doctors what I saw here? You're calm now," he said, reinforcing her more rational behavior, "and you're talking rationally about what any person would want. You want to see your kids and sleep in your own bed. That doesn't sound crazy to me." When he said that, he was again reflecting back what the woman had told him initially. He was also normalizing, not criticizing, her point of view. He didn't think about it; he just naturally did it because he was so well practiced at using the reflective listening tool. She looked grateful and said, "You would do that for me?"

"Absolutely," he answered.

"But how do I know my husband will let me in afterward?"

"I'll ask him," he said. And, in her presence, he used his cell phone to call her husband. The conversation lasted less than a minute. After he ended the call, he turned to the woman and said, "Your husband says if you go to the hospital and the doctor says you're okay to come home, he promises to let you in, and I believe he'll keep his word. So, what would you like to do?"

"I'll go," she answered, "but only with you in your car."

The sergeant told me afterward that this entire interaction, from the initial standoff, when the woman was yelling and refusing to speak with the police, to her quietly getting into the backseat of his squad car, took less than fifteen minutes.

> Learning to partner is really about getting to the core of what matters most to *both* of you and finding a way to make that happen without getting sidetracked by the impasse.

When they got to the hospital, Sergeant Scott kept his promise and spoke to the doctor. He really did think the woman was mentally ill, but she had been acting more rationally after she calmed down, and he empathized with her natural desire to go home and see her kids. He was honest both with her and with the doctor. But he also described her appearance and behavior when the police first arrived on the scene. Because the doctor already knew her history of bipolar disorder and because she was showing symptoms of mania, he admitted her to the hospital, which was precisely what her husband had been counting on.

NOTICE THAT NO ONE in any of these situations got to hear the other say "you're right," and no one person "won." Learning to partner is really about getting to the core of what matters most to *both* of you and finding a way to make that happen without getting sidetracked by the impasse.

PART THREE

LEAP for
the Many Faces
of Impasse

11

LEAP to Better
Relationships at Home

If they were right I'd agree.
But it's them they know, not me.
Now there's a way and I know that I have to go away.
I know I have to go.

—Cat Stevens, "Father and Son"

In this chapter and the ones that follow, I'll be giving you a picture of what LEAP looks like in different scenarios. These stories will show you how the tools you've already acquired can be used together in real-life situations. As you'll see, it isn't necessary to use every tool in every situation, and sometimes the order in which you use them will change. But the basic principles of disarming, befriending, finding common ground, and working together from that common ground will be obvious in each story you read. By seeing how others have used these tools you will discover your own rhythm—those styles of using LEAP that fit your personality and feel right to you—and become more adept at using all the tools in your belt.

AS YOU KNOW, LEAP is first and foremost about preserving relationships—without that, you cannot move past an impasse. So what better place to start looking at how relationships can be either damaged or strengthened than within your own family? If you blow up at and blow off a customer service rep on the telephone, you may be making it more difficult to get what you need from him, but you'll probably never talk to him again. In fact, you can just hang up, hit re-dial, and start afresh with another person. But you only have one fam-ily, so maintaining loving relationships with your family members may be the most important reason of all to use LEAP. In this chapter we'll be looking at three situations—parent and child, husband and wife, and adult siblings caring for aging parents.

When Your Son Wants to Be a Rock Star

Jim and Liz were beside themselves. Their sixteen-year-old son, Ben, was about to flunk out of school and he couldn't have cared less. For the past six months he hadn't done his homework, he was skipping classes whenever he could, and when he couldn't, according to his teachers, he spent the entire period staring out the window or into space. Nothing his parents had said or done so far had even gotten him to admit there was a problem. All he ever said was that school was "boring" and he didn't want to go to college anyway, so what did it matter if he flunked out. His par-ents, both of whom were college educated and completely convinced of the advantages of education, were horrified and furious. But the more they screamed, the less Ben listened, until he finally refused to discuss the situation at all. At that point they figured LEAP was their last chance to get through to him, so they might as well give it a try.

Once again they sat down with him to try to make him see things their way, only this time they were determined to do it differ-ently. First of all, they decided that Jim would talk to Ben alone so Ben wouldn't feel like his parents were ganging up on him.

Ben, of course, started out defensively, as usual. "I don't know why you want to talk about this. You don't care what I think anyway. You just want me to keep going to school and not get thrown out. I'll go, but I already told you, I don't care about school. It's boring!"

This time, however, Jim refused to take the bait. He didn't tell Ben that he *needed* to care about school because school was important. That was his agenda, but it clearly wasn't Ben's. Instead he said, "Okay, Ben. I understand. School isn't important to you because it's boring and you don't want to go to college anyway, have I got that right?"

"Yeah," he said sullenly, but at least he was responding. "It's a huge waste of time. Do we have to talk about this? You're just going to yell at me. This is a waste of time, too."

Refusing to take the bait and argue, Jim said, "Yes, we do, but I swear I won't yell at you. I want to know if you feel like I at least understand your position. You said school's boring, a waste of time, and you're not going to college anyway, right?" Jim asked neutrally without an ounce of challenge or sarcasm in his voice.

"Yeah, I guess so," Ben said noncommittally.

"Well, is that your view or not, Ben?" Jim persisted.

"Yes! All right! You get it."

"Good. So I *do* understand," Jim said without reacting to the angry outburst. "Now, what I'd really like to know, if you don't mind telling me, is *why* you don't want to go to college."

His father had never asked him that before, so Ben was naturally a little suspicious, but he figured he'd go along with it—for now. "I told you. Classes are boring. So if high school is boring, why would I want to go on to college?"

"Uh-huh. That makes sense. I suppose I would feel the same way about college if I were in your shoes."

"What? You would?"

"Sure. If high school is boring, why should college be any different?"

"So you're not going to give me a hard time about not going to college? You agree with me?" Ben asked, confused.

"My answer to the first question is no. I am not going to give you a hard time about this anymore. But I really don't want to answer the second question just yet because there are some more things I'd like to know. Is that okay?"

"I guess so. Like, what do you want to know?"

"For starters, could you tell me what you think you *do* want to do that wouldn't be so boring?" Jim was being careful to not let any hint of sarcasm creep into his voice. It wasn't easy because he felt the strong impulse to say something else, such as, "You're just a kid and you don't have a clue what you're talking about! It's stupid to not go to college. You'll go and that's that. Believe me, you'll thank me when you're older." But he didn't say any of these things because he knew strong-arming Ben hadn't worked in the past and that this might be his last chance to get through to him before it was too late.

Ben was curious now. His father was actually asking him what he wanted to do instead of telling him what he *should* do, and it even sounded like he might be willing to listen. But he still didn't think his dad was going to like what he had to say. "I want to play in my band," he almost whispered.

Jim knew, of course, that Ben was playing guitar and singing in a band along with his friend Max. They played at school parties and had already burned two amateur CDs, which they sold at their gigs and on the band's Web site. Ben and Max also wrote the songs their band played. But in Jim's mind, Max was part of the problem. He was twenty years old and a high school dropout. Obviously he was a bad influence on Ben.

Ben was actually an outstanding musician and budding song-writer. He spent countless hours practicing and writing and the results were impressive. In fact, a local college radio station had begun to play one of their songs regularly. When Ben had first picked up the guitar, Jim and Liz were proud of him and encouraged his playing. Later, they even bought copies of the band's CDs to give to friends and family. But when they realized it was taking up so much of his time, that he'd dropped off the swim team and was cutting basketball practice to attend rehearsals, they were sorry they'd ever encouraged him at all.

This time, however, Jim knew better than to say, "But don't you think that graduating from high school is more important right now?" That "but," he knew, would just get Ben all cranked up again, and they seemed to be making some progress—at least Ben was talking to him, rather than just at him. So instead, he continued to follow his son's lead, nodding and asking, "So do you and Max have a plan for the band? I mean, like a one-, two-, or three-year plan?"

"You're not going to understand." Ben sighed, sounding defeated.

"Hey, I'm listening, aren't I?" Ben nodded, and Jim asked, "Do you think I understand your opinion about high school and college?"

"I guess so."

"So give me a chance. We've never talked about where you see this thing going and, like I said, I'm not going to keep pushing college on you."

"We want to get an apartment in Manhattan, in the East Village, and start playing in the city," Ben said all in a rush, waiting for his dad to explode.

"Oh, an apartment in the East Village, eh? And just how are you going to afford that?" Jim shot back, reflexively falling into his old bad habits.

"I knew I shouldn't have talked to you about this!" was Ben's equally knee-jerk response.

"No, wait. I'm sorry. I was wrong. I'm not perfect. Okay?" Jim caught himself, realizing as he heard his son's defenses go up that he had *reacted* to what Ben had said rather than *reflecting* it.

"Okay," Ben said, clearly suspicious again.

"But it will cost a lot to live there, won't it?" Jim tried again.

"Yeah, Dad, I'm not an idiot. I know it'll be expensive."

"Hey, I never called you an idiot, and I said I was sorry. My question is, have you guys figured out how you're going to be able to afford it?"

Actually, Ben and Max had not figured out how to finance their plan, and that fact provided an important opening for Jim and Liz to get what they needed.

"So, Ben," Jim began, "it sounds like you're going to need a little help getting started."

At that, Ben just shrugged.

Jim plunged ahead. "I can certainly understand your wanting to move to the city. That's where all the action is and, if I were you, I'd probably want to do exactly the same thing."

"Yeah, right." Ben laughed, mocking his father. "You graduated top in your class and went straight through to college. You would never do anything like this."

"I didn't say I would do it."

"Yes, you did!" Ben said, raising his voice. "You *just* said that!"

"Can I explain?" Jim asked, remembering to ask questions.

"Go ahead, but that's what you said."

"I won't argue with you about what I did or didn't say, but I can tell you what I meant to say. I understand why you want to do it. That's what I meant by saying if I were you I would want to do the same thing."

"Yeah, but you're not me and you don't approve."

"Actually, whether I approve or not isn't important. I mean, I would like my opinion to matter to you, but the fact is the decision is going to be yours. And even if I don't necessarily agree with all of it, I can try and understand and respect it."

Visibly more relaxed, Ben said, "So you're saying that you can see— you get it—why I want to move into the city, right?"

"That's right," Jim said, smiling inwardly at the fact Ben had just unconsciously copied Jim's strategy of listening reflectively.

"That's rad," Ben said, clearly pleased. "Mom won't ever get it, though."

Ignoring the question of whether Liz would see it Ben's way or not, Jim pushed on. "Sure, what musician wouldn't want to be in a place with all those clubs and where all those music videos are getting shot all the time? I'm not completely *old school*, you know!"

"But you still think I should go to college, right? You still think I'm wrong about that."

Mentally reaching for his A tools, Jim answered, "Well, Ben, since you ask, and I'm really sorry because I think what I'm about to say is going to make you angry again, and I could be wrong, but, yeah, I do think getting a college education is important, so I hope we can just agree to disagree on that. You don't think it's important and I can respect that even if I don't share your view. Can you respect my opinion?"

"When you put it that way, yeah. At least you're not shoving it down my throat."

"I don't want to do that. Can I ask you another question?" Jim asked.

"Yeah."

"I wonder if there may be a way for you to move to the city, work on your music, *and* go to college. Maybe if you were studying something you *are* interested in you wouldn't think it was so boring. Do you think that's possible?"

"Like what?" Ben asked.

"Music."

"I took music and it sucked, Dad. I learned more from Max and the guys in the first week we played together than I ever learned in two years of music classes in high school."

"I can believe that," Jim agreed, before adding, "Are music classes in college, I mean in those colleges that offer music programs, the same as what you had in high school?"

"I don't know," Ben admitted.

"Do you think we could check it out together? Maybe go online and see what's available? You could also ask Max."

Ben agreed to all three suggestions and discovered there was a music program his friend Max would have "killed to get into" that fit right in with Ben's dreams for himself. After Ben had shared this information with his father, Jim spoke with his wife and came back with an offer. "So," he said to his son, "what if I told you your mother and I would be willing to pay for your apartment *and* pay your college tuition if you'd just be willing to enroll in this school and take liberal arts classes at the same time. They have that combined track according to the Web site you showed me." Now, this sounds a lot like bribery on the face of it, but it's really just a proposal for a partnership that addresses the shared interests of the negotiating parties. In fact, Jim and Liz had talked about helping Ben out regardless of whether he went to college. But because they had an agenda, too—they still wanted him to get a college degree—they made sure their first offer addressed everyone's needs. Apparently, Ben didn't see it as bribery. He looked surprised but excited about his parents' offer and asked, "Are you serious?"

"Absolutely," Jim answered.

"But my grades suck. How do you know I'd even get in?"

"Well, Ben, I know you're smart, and I know if you tried you could bring those grades back up. Maybe you can stop saying 'suck' all the time, too!" Ben laughed with his father at that observation. "I also know you're a great musician and I think any music school would be lucky to have you. So, what do you think? Could you give it a shot?"

Ben agreed, and now that he had a reason that motivated *him* to do better in school, he was able to improve his grades. Because he was planning to apply to a music program, his experience with the band actually worked to his benefit far more than remaining on the swim or basketball team would have done. And as he focused more on his grades, he naturally spent a little less time with the band. This happened all on its own without anyones' telling him it was a good idea to cut back on practicing. In the end, he was accepted to college and in the liberal arts–music track. Today he's a motivated student well on his way to a successful career in music, and his parents are confident he'll finish college and get the degree that's so important to *them*.

When Kids Come Between You

Helen and Daryl both loved their daughters and wanted only the best for them, but they couldn't see eye to eye on what that meant in terms of their education. Helen wanted them to attend an all-girls private school run by the church she attended. Daryl disagreed for a number of reasons that for a long time remained unspoken because he and Helen could never get past arguing about whether they could afford the tuition. Their situation provides a clear example of how getting stuck in an impasse can shut down communication, even between people whose relationship is loving and trusting.

ACCORDING TO HELEN, every time she brought up the subject of private school, Daryl would counter with, "We can't afford it," and their argument would then go something like this:

"Yes, we can! We don't need to buy a new car this year. We could use that money to cover the girls' tuition."

"First of all, we don't have that money. We'd be taking out a loan to buy that car. Second of all, even if we did have the money for the first year in hand right now, what would we do next year and the year after that?"

"We could remortgage the house *and* hold off on getting a new car. Then we'd have tuition money for several years at least."

"Helen, we need a new car. It can't wait."

"That's ridiculous. Our old car is perfectly fine. You just want all those new gadgets—the GPS and satellite radio and all that junk."

"You don't know what you're talking about."

"Yes, I do. The girls aren't getting what they need in public school and they're exposed to a lot of bad influences. Clearly, having a new car is more important to you than your daughters' education."

"Public school was good enough for you and me and it's good enough for the girls!"

Notice that not once in this exchange (or the many others just like it) did either one of them reflect back what he or she had heard the other say. Instead, each was *reacting* to what the other said (Helen doesn't know what she's talking about and Daryl cares more about his new car than his daughters' education) until the argument escalated and ultimately ended in an impasse.

When I met with Helen, it became clear that she did, in fact, know what she was talking about and that she and Daryl could very well afford to send their children to the private school Helen wanted them to attend. She explained that they both had secure high-paying jobs, almost no debt, and nearly 80 percent equity in their house. Only 20 percent of that equity would be needed to cover the girls' tuition for the full term of their enrollment. Moreover, she wasn't convinced they even had to refinance—this was her backup plan—and could handle the tuition by cutting back on a few things, like a new car. Once I understood that much, I helped her to learn that the new car and ability to pay the tuition were never really the issue and encouraged her to stop arguing about that. I coached her in the art of reflective listening so she would be able to go back and broach the subject again, this time armed with the tools she'd need to lower her husband's defenses, learn what his resistance was really about, and find a solution.

When she next brought up the idea, she didn't go on the attack, reiterating that they could very well afford the tuition. Instead she began by saying, "I understand what you said, that we can't afford it, and I'd really like to know more about *why* that is. I promise I'll listen and I'm not going to tell you we *can* afford it."

Her strategy was to disarm Daryl and make him understand that she really did respect his opinion. Once she did that, he no longer felt the need to defend his being worried, and, as a result, he was able to discuss the money issue without getting hot under the collar. That, in turn, freed them to look for common ground and really try to solve their problem. Helen suggested that if they mortgaged the house they could probably buy the new car *and* send the girls to private school, because they'd also be getting a tax deduction on the interest they'd be paying. Daryl had to agree that this was a good suggestion, and, in fact, the more they talked, the more he was able to talk himself out of his money worries. Finally, Helen was able to say, "So then you agree we can do it, right?"

But, as it turned out, Daryl wasn't yet able to agree because, as is so often the case, what they'd been arguing about wasn't really the problem at all. His reply to Helen's question was, "Well, I'm still not really comfortable with this." And when she asked why, his initial response was, "I'm not sure." But very quickly he took that back, saying, "No, I do know why," and that's when they were finally able to talk about what had been the real stumbling block.

Daryl didn't attend Helen's church and he was truly afraid that if his daughters attended the church school they would be taught to believe their father was a sinner and damned to go to hell. "I don't think *you* believe that," he said, "but it's what they'll be taught in that school, and I really don't want to spend my money so that my children can be educated to believe I'm a sinner."

When she heard what had *really* been troubling him all along, Helen said, "Oh, my God, I had no idea you—"

"How can you have no idea?" he interrupted. "It's what they teach! Remember, I tried it out when we first got married and the message was clear, 'It's our way or there's hell to pay.'"

"That's not fair," Helen said, getting defensive. "I have never said anything like that and you know I don't believe it."

"You're right and I'm not saying you have—but they do and I don't want my kids learning that. It makes me really mad when I think of them learning that."

"I can see why you feel angry about that. I would, too," she said empathetically.

Now that she finally understood why Daryl had been against the school—and why he was so quick to anger whenever they tried to talk about it—she was able to reassure him. She told him she didn't believe he was going to hell and it would never be acceptable to her for their daughters to be taught that. "No wonder you were so against this," she said. "I'm sorry to say I didn't think about this. I love that church but certain things I just tune out. There must be something we can do to ensure they don't get exposed to that message."

Now they had really found common ground, something they could agree on wholeheartedly. And they worked together to come up with a plan for making sure the girls were exposed to other religions and understood their parents' beliefs on the subject of Daryl going to hell simply because he didn't belong to a particular religion. Finally, Daryl felt comfortable enough to give it a try.

Once Daryl felt his opinion was truly being heard and respected, he let go of his defenses, and when he did that he was able to stop defending a position he didn't really hold in the first place (that they couldn't afford the private school) and allow himself to be honest and open about what was actually bothering him. That, in turn, opened the door for him and Helen to reach an agreement and work together to solve the real problem, which was one neither of them wanted to have.

I can't stress how important it is to learn to distinguish between what you think you *want* and what you really *need*. In this case, Helen thought she wanted to convince Daryl they could afford the school tuition, and Daryl, equally wholeheartedly, wanted to convince her they couldn't. It was only when they were able to stop fighting about the money (which was actually a red herring) that they could listen to one another, discover the real issue, and find a way to get what they both needed. For Helen that was a good education for their daughters; for Daryl it was the assurance that they wouldn't be educated (or, as he would put it, brainwashed) into believing their daddy was a sinner.

When Siblings Are Estranged

Stephanie and Josh are sister and brother. They'd always been close, but when it came time to decide how to take care of their aging parents they almost lost one another. Their father, who was in his eighties, had been diagnosed with Alzheimer's and their mother, in her mid-seventies, had recently suffered a heart attack. The couple could no longer care for one another, and they couldn't afford to pay for the care they would need to stay in their own home. The difficult question Stephanie and Josh had to decide was whether their parents should go into a nursing home or live with one of their children. Making these decisions isn't easy in the best of circumstances, but every time Stephanie and Josh got together, their discussion quickly escalated into a toxic argument.

JOSH WAS ADAMANT: "Either they live with you or they go to a nursing home."

"How can you even suggest that?" Stephanie would counter. "I could never live with myself if I dropped them off in a nursing home."

"I guess you're a better person than I am."

"That's not fair!"

"Why don't you just say it, Steph? I'm not a good son, I don't love Mom and Dad."

"That's not what I said! You're such a victim!"

"Like hell it isn't! And if anyone's a victim, it's you," Josh said, taking the bait.

And so it would go until, one day, Stephanie just said, "Well, then, forget it. They're coming to live with me. I can't keep arguing with you about this."

> In the heat of the battle, we start seeing demons that are not there. We not only lose sight of the big picture, we also lose sight of who our opponent really is.

The problem was that because she was so furious and accusations were flying, Stephanie found herself thinking maybe Josh didn't love their parents as much as he should. Obviously Josh was picking up on this change in her view of him and was defending himself against the accusation, even though she had not made it explicitly. The odd thing is she never before thought that, as Josh had always been a loving son. All she could figure was that her resentment had simmered to the point that she found herself believing, if for only brief moments, something she didn't truly believe deep down inside. In the heat of the battle, we start seeing demons that are not there. We not only lose sight of the big picture, we also lose sight of who our opponent really is.

Stephanie never got around to listening to Josh and maybe finding out why it was that their parents couldn't live with him even part of the time. Knowing him as well as she did, she should have guessed it couldn't simply be that he didn't love them. But having, in effect, dealt with the impasse by thumbing her nose at him, she then began to resent the burden she'd shouldered and was getting angrier and angrier with her brother, to the point where they were hardly speaking to one another.

Now they were both going it alone. Stephanie had unilaterally appointed herself sole caregiver, and Josh was finding it difficult even to visit his parents in his sister's home. In fact, every time he did visit, the tension was so thick you could cut it with a knife.

Neither of them had wanted it to be this way. But by breaking the impasse in the way she did, Stephanie ensured she wouldn't get what she needed—her brother's participation and help. She also missed him, and as time went on she realized that if they were ever going to become reconciled, she would have to make the first move. We'll be talking in detail about how to open closed doors in chapter 15, but what Stephanie did was to send Josh an e-mail apologizing for what had gone between them and admitting she might have been wrong. She also let him know she respected his opinion and promised that if he agreed to speak with her she would listen and not tell him he was wrong ever again.

Josh had been lonely, too. He felt as if he had lost his entire family, and he was willing to take the chance that Stephanie really meant what she'd said, so he agreed to talk with her.

"Josh," she said. "I know you feel our parents can't live with you and I really would like to know why. I know you love them, and I promise to listen to your reasons and not argue with you or tell you you're wrong to feel this way."

This is just what Josh had been longing to hear all along. Now, because he didn't have to defend against the accusation that he didn't love his parents, he was comfortable enough to be open and honest with his sister for the first time. He said, "I'm glad you realize that I love Mom and Dad as much as you do and that I wish I could have them live with me. But the fact is this: My marriage is nearly dead and bringing them into our home would be like hammering the last nail into the coffin. I was just not ready—and I'm still not—to give up on my marriage, so I had to say no."

By that point in the conversation Stephanie was near tears. She didn't even have to think about empathizing with her brother because her heart truly went out to him. Moreover, she realized that because their conversations about how to take care of their parents had always turned toxic so quickly, she'd never given him the opportunity to explain the reason for his resistance to helping out in the way she wanted him to. "I'm so sorry about your marriage. I had no idea. You must feel so sad," she said. Josh admitted to feeling depressed, and the two of them talked about what had been happening in his marriage and how much they had missed one another.

Now that their defenses were down, Stephanie was able to admit that she really did need her brother's help and Josh was able to have a conversation with her that focused on finding ways for both of them to get what they needed. They agreed they wanted to be there for one another and for their parents, and, based on that, they were able to figure out ways for Josh to take more responsibility for their care without involving his wife or actually having them live in his house. It was his idea to spend Sundays with them at Stephanie's house so she could have the day off. He also offered to pay for an aide to relieve his sister four evenings a week. Stephanie was grateful and, more important, brother and sister were again on good terms.

The Truth Is the Key to Being Trustworthy

In every one of these scenarios the people who were arguing really loved one another very much, and yet the toxicity of their arguments came dangerously close to ruining their relationships, perhaps beyond repair. In each one of these stories loved ones began to lose sight of who they were arguing with and saw demons that were not really there. Stephanie saw a selfish brother who did not love their parents, Daryl saw a Bible-thumping wife who did not care if their daughters thought poorly of a sinful father, and Ben saw dogmatic parents who could never understand or appreciate his desires.

When you're stuck in an impasse and bitter words are spewing poison into the air, chances are you've also lost sight of what you were actually arguing about or you were never able to see it in the first place. When you use the tools LEAP provides, you'll find that there will come an almost magical breakthrough moment when defenses are down and the truth can be revealed.

People are often afraid of the truth and hide it from the person with whom they are arguing. But almost as often, as Daryl discovered, they hide it from themselves. Yet knowing and speaking the truth is the key to establishing your credibility. It is the key to becoming trustworthy. And only by becoming worthy of the other person's trust will you be able to ask for, and get, her help.

Knowing and speaking the truth is the key to establishing your credibility. It is the key to becoming trustworthy.

What important truths did the family members in these scenarios reveal about themselves? I think they can all be summarized in one word, "vulnerability." Jim admitted to his son, Ben, that he could and did make mistakes—he was only human. Josh revealed to his sister that he was feeling overwhelmed by anxiety and sadness because of his failing marriage. Daryl was afraid of being rejected by his own daughters.

Gerry Spence, the trial lawyer and author, once told me about his first lesson in the power of making yourself vulnerable—baring all—to another person. I was astounded because, like Mr. Spence, I'd learned the same lesson in exactly the same way when I was five years old. My first girlfriend, Jenny, also five years old, lived next door. Behind my house was an unused barn we often played in. One day I asked Jenny to show me hers.

"I'm not going to show you mine!" she squealed, shocked but giggling.

"If I show you mine will you show me yours?" I persisted, dying to know if what my older brother had told me about the differences between boys and girls was true.

"You'll show me yours first?" she asked, now clearly curious.

"Yes!" I said, excited.

"Cross your heart and hope to die?"

"Cross my heart and hope to die, stick a needle in my eye."

"Okay," she said.

And so I did, and so did she.

When we reveal ourselves, our underbelly, so to speak, people feel safer and more willing to do the same. There is actually a lot of research on this subject. Social psychologists have shown in study after study that self-disclosure breeds self-disclosure. In other words, if you reveal your true self, especially your vulnerabilities, other people will usually do the same. One reason for this, I believe, is that in addition to feeling safer with someone who is being truthful and vulnerable, we also feel a desire to help and even protect that person.

You have to give in order to receive. What the LEAP-skilled people in the stories you just read gave was not only their ear, their respect, and their empathy, but also their vulnerability—the truth of how they were feeling. And for that, they got the same in return. Once both parties felt trust, and trusted, solutions were easy to find.

12

LEAP to Better
Business Relations

The greatest change in corporate culture—and the way business is being conducted—may be the accelerated growth of relationships based . . . on partnership.

—Peter F. Drucker

All businesses are profit-driven. Even a not-for-profit business is in the game of amassing more dollars for its cause. Think about what you believe to be the one most basic contributor to the profitability of any business. Is it the physical plant? The latest technology? The quality of the product or service provided?

No.

It's relationships.

Relationships are central to the workplace. Without productive relationships among colleagues and between suppliers and clients, no business can exist, much less turn a profit. I won't defend this proposition by citing all the authors of best-selling books on business who agree with me, or authoritative treatises on the subject, because I think it's as plain as the nose on your face. Without productive—I would argue collaborative—relationships, profit is impossible.

There have been a lot of books lately that focus on how to "handle" difficult people. There are, in fact, difficult people out there. But these books make the common mistake of focusing solely on problem people instead of problem relationships. When you focus on what's wrong with a person, you are not paying attention to what's wrong with the relationship you have with that person and, most important, those things you can do differently to make your relationship more collaborative and, consequently, more productive—even if the person is still difficult. Simply by paying attention to whether your disagreement with a coworker, boss, employee, or client has turned you into adversaries, you will be able to halt the downward spiral and use the LEAP tools you have learned to turn your relationship into one marked by mutual respect, curiosity, openness, trust, and a desire to find a solution that benefits you both. You can transform it from one that diminishes personal satisfaction and bleeds red ink into one that enhances quality of life and creates a healthy bottom line.

THE TAX MAN

Noah, the CEO of a boat-building company, had just hung up the phone with the mayor of the town in which his largest and most profitable factory was located and where he had been planning to expand his business. We'll call him Mayor McCartney. The mayor had called to tell Noah the city council was proposing a 30 percent increase in the factory's property taxes and that he was inclined to go along with it. The decision was made at the last closed city council meeting without any input from Noah. The town was in trouble financially and looking for a quick fix, so they turned to the most profitable business in town for the solution.

CAUGHT OFF GUARD by the call, Noah's knee-jerk reaction was to immediately threaten the mayor with dire consequences. "You know, this tax—coming out of the blue like this—would force me to lay people off. I'd have to save the money somewhere, and we are the largest employer in town. Maybe you ought to think about how this would affect the lives of your constituents, especially since this is an election year."

McCartney, quite naturally, met that threat with one of his own. "Well, Noah, you have to decide what's best for your business, but you must understand that this is going to make it very difficult for me to endorse the petition for a zoning variance you just filed." Noah was

about to meet that threat with another of his own—a hardball negotiating strategy—when he caught himself and realized he was about to
get into a head-butting match. Previous experience had taught him
that this mayor did not respond well to threats, and using this approach would lead nowhere but to an impasse that both he and the
mayor would probably live to regret. So he bit his tongue and remembered to BET. After taking a couple of deep breathes, he said, "Listen,
I'm really sorry but I'm in the middle of a meeting right now, and I
think it would be best if I called you back as soon as it's over. Would
that be acceptable?"

McCartney agreed, and with the time he had given himself to reflect, Noah decided to meet with the mayor in person. He called back
as promised and arranged the meeting for the following week. Seated
over a cup of coffee at a local diner they both frequented, he was prepared and mindful of the LEAP tools he had learned. He began by being honest about and apologizing for his initial reaction.

"I'm sorry I was so defensive. I was caught off guard, but that's no excuse for trying to strong-arm you. I hope you can accept my apology."

"Of course, Noah. No harm done," McCartney said with a small
sigh of relief.

"After we hung up I realized I don't really have a clue about the
thinking behind this proposal. Would you mind telling me why the city
council believes it's a good idea?"

"I'll be frank about this. As you must know, we've had to absorb
some unexpected expenses of our own. The floods we had last spring
left us way over budget in highway and drainage repairs, and, at the
same time, our fuel costs have skyrocketed. We had to look at all our
revenue options, and the fact is your company has experienced substantial growth this year. It's true you're the biggest employer in town,
but it's also true the town's been good to you. You're in the black and
looking to expand. I think the proposed increase is well within the
bounds of reason."

"*Hardly,*" Noah thought. "*It may be reasonable for you, but not for us!*"
What he said, however, was, "Just so I'm sure I'm straight about this,
the town has had several significant unforeseen expenses and, given

the fact that we've done well this year and would like to expand, we are a reasonable source of revenue to cover the shortfall. Is that about right?"

"So you see my point. I know you don't like it, but I think it's best for us all, wouldn't you agree?"

"Before I weigh in again, I'd like to hear a bit more. Is that okay?"

"What do you want to know?" McCartney asked, not sure what more there was to say.

"Well, I'd like to know, if you don't mind telling me, just how much over budget you actually are."

Notice that when Noah listened reflectively he did not react, omit anything, or defend himself in any way. And his opponent's nondefensive response was, as I would have predicted, a question about whether Noah now agreed. Noah most definitely did not think the tax increase was either fair or what was best for his company. He was reminded of a poster his secretary had framed on her wall: "Lack of planning on your part does not constitute an emergency on ours." But he also remembered, because he had mentally strapped on his LEAP tool belt, that expressing this sentiment would not get him what he needed.

What did he need? He needed first to preserve his relationship with the town, and he was already back on track in this regard. Now he needed Mayor McCartney to work with him. So, after delaying giving his opinion and getting more information about the budget shortfalls, Noah used the empathy tool.

"That budget meeting must have been sobering. If it were me, I would have lost some sleep over those figures," Noah said.

"You've got that right! I knew it was a bad year, but, yes, I was surprised by how bad it really was, and it hasn't helped my ulcer."

Notice that Noah asked about sadness and anxiety without actually using those words (he used "sobering" and "lost sleep" instead). That's acceptable and tells me he was tuned in to the mayor's feelings. Noah didn't think McCartney would have been receptive to hearing, "You must be depressed and scared about this," so he used substitutes. But even without using the words he thought would have been more apt, he got closer to his opponent's feelings and consequently to him. Then, believing the timing was right, he moved on to exploring where they might agree and where their shared interests lay.

"Can I tell you what I think about this?" Noah began, remembering to ask permission rather than just saying, "Here's what I think. . . ."

"Of course," McCartney replied.

"I think we both want the town's budget balanced. Right?" Again, Noah was speaking the truth because the healthier the town's finances were, the better it would be for his business. From repair of the roads he relied on to ship his boats to the quality of the schools his employees sent their children to, his fortunes were tied to the town's. "And we both want my factory to stay in the black, hire more people rather than laying anyone off, and complete our expansion. You agree?" he asked.

"Sure. But I don't see how we can get all that done," McCartney said, obviously skeptical. He still wasn't thinking beyond the original proposal. In his mind there were only two choices: Either the town had a budget shortfall or Noah's company—the most profitable local business by far—paid more taxes. But when he said, "I don't see how we can get all that done," he was implicitly inviting Noah to weigh in.

This was the first time Noah had any influence over the options on the table. And he was now in a good position to explore new ways in which he could partner with the town. Leaning across the table, he said, "I bet if we put our heads together we could come up with additional ways to offset the shortfall. What do you think?"

Noah got the mayor's agreement, and together, focusing on their shared interests, they came up with some novel ideas no one in the town government had previously considered. This is not a surprise, because no one in the government had been talking to Noah. Among the goals they partnered on was Noah's campaign to get one of his major suppliers to move his factory into town. He'd wanted this anyway to save shipping costs and increase efficiency, but now he saw that if he could seal that deal the town would get much of the increase in tax revenue they needed from someone other than him. Together the mayor and Noah put together an incentive package and presented it to the supplier, who was impressed enough to make the commitment they both sought.

But that was only one of several options they were able to come up with. Noah's company made a substantial contribution to the school district to build a new facility. The contribution not only created a great deal of goodwill, but it was equal to only two years' worth of the original proposed tax increase. From Noah's perspective the donation was a "no-brainer" and far cheaper than the alternative. They also agreed on a modest 5 percent tax increase, one Noah could easily live with. Noah convinced the town that the more modest tax increase could be spread among all the businesses in town without much resistance from the small business owners. He was right. None of the options they part-nered on would have been possible if Noah hadn't stopped threatening McCartney and trying to convince him he was wrong to raise the com-pany's taxes. As or more important than the tax savings, however, was the fact that Noah had preserved and strengthened his relationship with the mayor and the town. In fact, based on that collaboration, Noah became an especially trusted and valued member of the community. From then on the mayor and some of the city council members began to consult with him on matters that concerned his business—and sometimes even on issues that had nothing to do with him directly.

She's So Wrong, but So What?

I employ a group of psychologists who conduct psychological fitness evaluations for a range of companies. I design the assessments, supervise the evaluations, and coauthor all the reports. One day I got a call from one of the executives with whom I had been corresponding via e-mail. We have worked together for several years and over the course of that time have become friends. We'll call her Sandy. Sandy was convinced I had not sent her two important reports she needed. I knew I had. She was wrong.

I ANSWERED THE phone on the first ring. "You didn't send me the revised reports you promised," Sandy said in answer to my hello.

"Are you sure?" I asked. "I just sent them to you this morning."

"No," she said. "What you sent me was exactly the same version you sent me before."

"Really? Would you mind doing me a favor and just checking the date of the file?"

"How do I do that?"

"Right click on the file icon, choose Properties, and look at the date the report was last modified." She agreed to do this, and a few clicks and taps later she said, "It doesn't give me that when I click Properties." .

"There's no date listed there?"

"No. You sent me the old one."

At that point, because I knew she was relatively computer illiterate, I was certain she was opening the old report and not the one I had just sent her, and so I pressed forward with proving I was right. "Hold on, I'm going to open the copy that's in my Sent e-mail folder." I did, and confirmed that what I had sent her that morning was indeed the revised report. I had incontrovertible proof she was wrong! There was no longer any doubt in my mind. So, because I was irritated and had tunnel vision, I told her—I am so smart sometimes.

"Sandy, I am a hundred percent certain you have the new, final version. I just checked and there's no way you have the first draft."

"Look, I know what I have here!" *Odd, she sounded far from pleased with my having solved the question of who was right.* "This is the old version. I need the new one now!"

Why was I doing this? What had I accomplished up to this point? All I had done was to make her defensive and angry. From Sandy's perspective I had not only sent the wrong report, I was now blaming her for my mistake and suggesting she was incompetent!

If you feel inclined to come to my defense, you might be thinking I had to correct her impression that *I* had acted incompetently. I had to let her know I had not, as she claimed, sent her the wrong file. It would be nice of you to think that, but I would have to disagree. If I had not lost the forest for the trees—because my thinking brain had momentarily shut down—I would have known she thought highly of me. We had several years of working together under our belts. Each of us considered the other highly competent. I didn't need to defend myself and I didn't need to be right.

But it wasn't until I felt the impasse growing that I stopped and thought about the bigger picture: *"Sandy likes me and thinks very highly of my work."* At that moment I realized my folly and remembered to use LEAP.

"Sandy, let me start over. You've checked and it's clear I didn't send you the revised report? Is that the bottom line?"

"That's what I've been trying to tell you!" she said, exasperated.

"Okay, then. I'm sorry. I'll send it right now."

"Thanks. So what are you doing this weekend?" she said, suddenly sounding as warm and friendly as she usually does.

In this situation, I remembered to take the temperature of the argument, shut down my emotional brain by thinking of the bigger picture, and use only the reflective listening and apology tools to break the ridiculous impasse I had been creating. By stepping back and calming down I immediately recognized what I really needed. That's why I was able to so easily let go of my single-minded quest to prove her wrong. It really was that simple.

The "I Can't Play Favorites" Excuse

Hilda's job required her to travel every week to meet with clients in the Pacific Northwest region of the United States. Like the other regional managers, she was based in Atlanta, but she traveled greater distances and more frequently than the others. Company policy was to reimburse employee travel expenses very quickly—usually, but not always, within thirty days. Hilda, however, had a problem with that policy and wanted a company credit card so she wouldn't have to ever wait to be reimbursed. She went to her boss, Mike, and made her request while he was sitting at his desk, tapping away on his computer keyboard.

LOOKING UP, MIKE said without skipping a beat, "None of the regional managers has a company card, Hilda. I can't play favorites."

"But you have your own card," she countered.

"All the vice presidents have cards, but no one at your level does. I'm sorry, but I just can't do it."

"That hardly seems fair. I travel far more than you or any of the other VPs, I'm paid less, and yet I have to float my expenses for the company. Does that seem fair to you?" she asked, making what I call the fairness argument and spicing it up with a little guilt.

Turning back to his computer screen, as if to signal that as far as he was concerned the conversation was over, Mike said, "Look, this is not about being fair. No is no. You'll just have to live with it."

Realizing she had irritated her boss, Hilda took her cue and left his office. But she didn't forget about what she still thought was an unfair company policy. About a month later, when she and Mike were at a sales conference in another city, she brought it up again. This time they were meeting over a cup of coffee to talk about one of her clients, and she had his full attention. When they had completed their other business she said, "Can I ask you something?"

"About what?"

"Remember when I asked you about getting a credit card?"

"Yes, I remember. Look, you did a great job with this client. Really great. I would love to get you a card but I can't appear to play favorites. You understand that, don't you?"

"Of course. But can I ask you something else?"

"What?"

"If we just imagined for a minute that I had a card, who do you suppose would be upset about it?"

"The other four regional managers, that's who," Mike said at once.

"You seem a little irritated that I'm bringing this up again. Are you?"

"Well, not irritated, but put off, yes. I've already told you that you've been doing great, but I just can't do anything about getting you a company card. My hands are tied."

Realizing that Mike was feeling a little guilty, perhaps as a result of what she'd said before about fairness, Hilda decided to reflect back what he had said and empathize rather than try to make him feel worse.

"If I understand your position, my getting a card doesn't have anything to do with my job performance. Right? It's apples and oranges."

"That's exactly right."

"I guess I would be a little irritated, too, if I were you, and I'm sorry to bring it up again. I just wanted to understand your position better."

"Look, I've told you already, my hands are tied."

"I know your hands are tied," Hilda reflected back, even though she knew they were not. He could give her a card if he wanted to; he just *thought* his hands were tied. "I'm not going to ask you again for the card, but I haven't really told you the reasons why I thought it would be okay for me to have one. Can I tell you now?"

"So long as you know I can't do anything about it, sure," Mike said, clearly more relaxed.

Having reflected back his point of view and empathized with how her request was making him feel, Hilda underscored what they agreed on. "First of all, I agree you can't play favorites and I would never dream of asking you to do that. I also agree I have to go through the ranks like you and everyone else did. I'm not a VP." She paused for effect, added, "Yet," and smiled.

"You're on track, though," Mike offered, also smiling.

"Thanks. What I was thinking is that even though I have the same title as the other RMs I have a very different travel schedule. I pulled their calendars off the network for the last quarter and found out that hour for hour I travel between twenty-five and forty percent more than anyone else. No one even comes close."

"I guess I'm not surprised, given your region and your motivation," Mike offered.

"Thanks again, but I actually was a little surprised by how much more it was, and so was the group."

"You told the other RMs?"

"When I mentioned that I was strapped for cash waiting for large reimbursements, they were supportive and suggested I ask you for a card. Actually, they gave me the idea in the first place."

"Do they know I said no to you?"

"I mentioned it, yes."

"I wish you'd asked me before you did that," Mike said, sounding a little peeved.

"How come?"

"I would have wanted to make sure they understood the reason I had to say no. In a way, it was for them."

Rather than responding defensively, Hilda continued to listen reflectively. "So you would have liked me to ask you first before telling them you'd refused so that you could explain your decision?"

"Yes."

"I'm sorry. For what it's worth, I told them what you told me, and we all agreed it made sense—all things being equal. But all things aren't equal because I am on the road much more than they are."

"I see your point. Let me think about this."

When they got back to the home office, Mike spoke with the other managers, who, as she'd said, all agreed that Hilda should have a company card and, moreover, let him know that none of them would feel he was playing favorites by giving her one.

The reason Hilda's second try at convincing Mike to see things her way was successful didn't rest on the merits of her argument. In fact, her argument wasn't any different from what it was the first time. She was successful because she stopped focusing on her position and put her effort into lowering Mike's defensiveness. When she listened and empathized with his position, he felt open to listening again to hers—for the first time really—and exploring his options. She created a working relationship with him that was independent of whether he agreed or disagreed with her position. As a result, Mike found a way to bend the rules. Policy and rules, from Mike's perspective, were to protect the company from the lowest common denominators—those employees who could not be counted on to perform at as high a level as Hilda. Once she had lowered Mike's defenses he was able to see the bigger picture and come to the conclusion that in her case, the rules should be bent, or more precisely, revised.

DAVID AND GOLIATH

When David told me he felt like he was battling Goliath, he was referring to the board of directors of the sports apparel and equipment com-

pany of which he was CEO. He had been hired by the board a year before with the mutual understanding that major changes needed to be made if the company was going to expand into international markets. But when he'd presented his five-year strategic plan at the last board meeting he was mercilessly attacked by the more senior members. He thought he might have allies but wasn't sure because he couldn't move the discussion past the impasse.

The plan seemed to be well received until he got to the proposal that they sell off their sports equipment division. He argued that they could use the proceeds from the sale to get endorsement contracts for their apparel and shoe divisions from top European and South American football (soccer) players and to fund both the advertising campaign and the infrastructure the new venture would require. The division they'd be selling had been losing money for the past six years, so it seemed the obvious choice. However, the president of the board, who was also the founder of the company, hated the idea.

"OUT OF THE question," he said. "That division is the backbone of this company. You're going to have to look elsewhere for the funds."

Two other long-standing board members immediately followed his lead. One went so far as to say, "This is irresponsible. We took a chance when we hired you, and this is the best you can come up with?" The other, also angry, said, "I don't think you have a clue what this company is about. What have you been doing this past year?" When they had finished, David was so insulted and angry he could barely speak. He addressed his response to the founder, who had at least not attacked him personally.

"Bernie, I thought we were serious about going multinational."

"What's that supposed to mean?" Bernie shot back.

Defending against the accusations that had been flung at him, David said, "This proposal was not invented this morning. It was carefully researched, and the least you can do is allow me to present its merits." Bernie agreed that they owed him at least that much and convinced the board to "hear David out."

Forty-five minutes later, when the PowerPoint slide show had ended and the lights were back up, David asked, "So, do you see now why I am proposing this?"

"David," Bernie said not unkindly, "I think I can speak for us all when I say, yes, I understand why you're proposing this. But there's something I don't think you understand. The sports equipment division is the heart and soul of this company. More than thirty years ago I started this company with our hiking and camping equipment lines. The first two years we were operating out of my basement and garage. Two of our employees in that division have been with me from the start. Even our company name has been with us since then. What's next? Are you going to suggest we change that, too?"

Actually, David had been thinking something along those lines—a modification of the existing name. But he had the good sense not to reveal those plans at this particular moment. Unfortunately, he still chose to stick with the substantive issues of his sell-off plan, basically reiterating all the arguments he had made during his slide presentation. Predictably, they fell on deaf ears.

The meeting ended in an impasse.

Next, David tried the divide-and-conquer approach. Over the next month he called or personally met with each board member separately. He argued his position admirably and convincingly. Had it been a debating competition he would have certainly won. But although his argument sounded convincing, David was not. He did not have the kind of working relationship with any of these people that he needed to sell his idea. In the end, all but one lined up behind Bernie.

David knew Bernie was the key, but he had all but given up on changing the founder's mind because he felt certain his position was emotionally based and not rational. He was half right. Bernie's position was imbued with a great deal of emotion—not that David understood it. But it was also rational, from Bernie's perspective. David needed to get inside Bernie's experience. Without knowing how the founder felt and thought, he would never break the impasse. And, just as important, without Bernie's trust, he could expect to find more impasses down the road.

David actually knew LEAP. In fact, he was a big fan of the method because it had helped him to break an impasse that had been destroying his relationship with his son. And yet, when it came to his impasse with the board of directors, he had never considered using the LEAP tools he'd acquired. It was as if he kept his tool belt locked up in a shed at home and never dreamed of taking it to work.

David still checks in with me periodically to tell me how he and his son are doing, and in the course of one of these conversations he told me about this workplace impasse. When I asked him if he had ever considered using LEAP with Bernie, he admitted he hadn't, but he was immediately eager to try. He decided to ask Bernie out to dinner. His goal for this meeting was nothing more than to learn about his perspective and perhaps gain some trust along the way. He went in planning not to mention his idea—even if Bernie tried to bring it up—and to focus instead on listening reflectively and strategically empathizing whenever it felt natural to do so.

Much of the dinner conversation was about family, sports, and other noncontroversial subjects, but as the dessert was served David said, "I'd like to talk to you about your reaction to my proposal. I was left with some questions after the last board meeting. Would that be all right?"

"What kind of questions? I think I was clear," Bernie said.

"Crystal!—and I don't want to talk about the proposal itself. But I realized after the meeting that I really know almost nothing about what went into starting this company. I was hoping you could give me some background." This was a subject Bernie could warm to, and for an hour they lingered over coffee as David listened attentively to Bernie's reminiscences of the company's first several years and the immense pride he took in realizing the potential of what he had begun. What he felt most proud of back then was the fact that dozens of families had relied on his business to pay mortgages, college tuition, and to get ahead in life, and he hadn't let them down. Even today he took more pride in the number of people "he" employed than the number of dollars he made.

David listened and learned. What's more, he reflected back what he was hearing and genuinely empathized with the happiness Bernie exuded when he talked about those early years. At one point Bernie asked, "You can see now why I can never sell off this division, can't you?"

From his own perspective, David couldn't see that at all. If Bernie supported David's plan, within a year he would be employing many more people than he was now. But from Bernie's perspective it made perfect sense. So David said, "I do see that. If I were you I couldn't part with it. It would be like betraying an old family friend who's always been there for you and now is counting on you to be there for him." When David said that it felt authentic, and he later told me, "I could see this light in the old man's eyes that I had never seen before. He reminded me of my father."

David still thought his plan was the right one for the company. But he had a richer understanding of the culture and value system that had originated with its founder. "The company" was more than shareholders and bottom lines. It had a palpable heartbeat that came from Bernie but echoed throughout the entire board and beyond. The best he could do to describe it was to say it was like the feeling a father has for his firstborn—a feeling of pride, protection, and loyalty. It was the reason the company had tolerated such excessive losses from this division, just as a father might help out a son who had fallen on hard times.

David, however, still needed the board's support to move forward. But now, mindful of the principles upon which LEAP is based, he no longer thought that digging in his heels and going to war with them would be fruitful. So, a week later, he met with Bernie again to talk about his strategic plan and how to fund the major initiatives that included the endorsement contracts and advertising. He began by saying, "I appreciate your meeting with me. I could use your input. It seems there's broad agreement on my plan as a whole but disagreement on how to fund it. I want to start with what we agree on. We agree that this strategic plan has a high likelihood of being successful, and we agree that we have the resources but not the liquidity to fund it." He then stopped and waited for Bernie to respond.

"Go on," he said.

"Before I do, am I mistaken, or do we agree on those points?"

"No, you are not mistaken." Bernie seemed to be steeling himself for the hard sell that never came.

Instead David asked, "What would you do if you were in my shoes?"

Bernie laughed and said, "I know where you're going with this."

Sitting back in his chair, David said, "I'm glad one of us does, because I don't! Truly, I'm stumped. After talking with you last week I've come to see some things your way. We can't just sell off the sports equipment division without betraying our most loyal employees and losing touch with our roots. I know I'm the new guy on the block, but I now see how important this is to you and everyone else around here. And I respect that."

Looking visibly relieved, Bernie sighed and said, "I appreciate that, David."

The two men then brainstormed for over an hour. Much of the ground they covered was the same as what David had covered months before during his presentation. But, in fact, this was the first time Bernie actually came to understand David's thought process, because he had been too angry to listen closely during the slide show. And because he was really listening, he came to see that their choices were fewer than he had supposed.

At the end of the meeting, Bernie suggested they continue the process by bringing in the other two senior board members who had reacted hostilely to David's proposal. When they met several days later David at first just listened respectfully to their suggestions, even when they were ideas he had already studied and rejected. Eventually, the work group reached a consensus. If they wanted to realize the strategic plan, their best option by far was to part with the division in question.

David then stirred things up by saying, "Maybe this isn't the time to expand internationally." Of course he really believed this was the right time, and the company's desire to go in that direction had been the main reason he took the job in the first place. But because he was approaching the negotiation from the perspective of the older board members, it was an honest, if implied, question. Of course, one of the board members asked him what *he* thought.

Using the delaying tool, he said, "Let me think about this some more before I answer, if you don't mind. There's a lot for me to process here."

No one pressed him, and when they all stood to leave at the end of the meeting, Bernie said, "I can see why you proposed this now. I still don't like it, but at least I understand that you didn't suggest it without giving it very careful thought."

David was able to answer honestly, "I don't like it either. At least not as much as I did." And he meant it. He felt the emotional ties these men had to the division and, more to the point, to the people who worked there. They agreed to meet again in one week.

David started this next meeting with the same provocative question, and the three older men all reaffirmed their commitment to taking the company international. They told him they had spoken together during the week and decided they needed to find a way to sell the equipment division without violating their ethics or damaging the reputation of the company. And they needed to address other concerns they had about both the employees who would be laid off and those who would be brought into the new effort. David was surprised they had come to this conclusion on their own, without any new arguments or case-making from him.

What had changed was not the force of David's argument; it wasn't his ideas that had won them over. Rather, it was the trust they had come to have in him. Bernie and the two other board members had now experienced David's listening to, respecting, and empathizing with their point of view. During the course of their meetings he had never once argued for his proposal. Even when they requested his opinion, he had respectfully asked if he could decline. The authors of *Getting to Yes* note that, "The human propensity for defensive and reactive behavior is one reason so many negotiations fail." I agree. By using LEAP, David was able to lower not only his own defenses but also those of his opponents.

Over the course of the next month he worked with his staff to put together a proposal for the sale that Bernie and the board could feel good about. In the end, acting as true partners, they sold the division in a manner that addressed their shared goals and interests.

The High Cost of
Not LEAPing in Business

What is the cost of a workplace impasse? Because it usually results in damage to relationships, the cost is very, very high. It can sometimes be calculated in terms of dollars lost, but that's not the worst of it. The impact on productivity, efficiency, morale, even health— don't forget sleep—and absenteeism is harder to calculate but easy to understand.

Too often, especially at work, we avoid conflict and either let an impasse stand or force a resolution that is not mutual. Bosses strong-arm their employees into accepting their viewpoint and end up with lowered morale and confidence. Employees become passive-aggressive with bosses and do end runs to get what they want. I am reminded of an acquaintance who could not convince his employer to give him a specific week off, even though he had accrued the vacation days. The next time he wanted time off, he took sick days rather than address the issue head-on. When a buyer feels cheated by a supplier or is forced to accept a deal he feels is unfair, he will take his pound of flesh in other ways.

Most of us spend more waking hours at work than we do with our loved ones, so having work relationships that are healthy and satisfying does much more than make us more productive, it makes us happier and healthier. Resolving workplace impasses by using LEAP will build mutual respect and trust—which is a far more desirable outcome than the alternative. And it will get you what you need most— a collaborative working relationship marked by mutual respect and appreciation.

13

Getting Service People
to LEAP to Your Assistance

*There is only one way under high heaven to get anybody to do
anything. Did you ever stop to think of that? Yes, just one way.
And that is by making the other person want to do it.*

—Dale Carnegie

How do you get other people to want to help you when it appears they
have little or no desire to do so? By transforming the nature of the relationship into one where that person feels appreciated and respected,
that's how. You may never have thought about forming a relationship
with the insurance company's representative on the other end of the
telephone or even with the pharmacist behind the counter at your local
drugstore. But when you need something from these people, the surest
way to get it is by finding a way for them to see you as an individual—one
they want to give to—not just another customer who's going to give them
a hard time and add more stress to an already stressful job. The way to
do that, as I described earlier, is to give something to them first.

Very few people call a service rep because they are happy with the
service. These calls are virtually always to complain. And the rep deals
with many of them every day—hour after hour after hour. The same is
true for the service people you encounter face-to-face. If the transaction goes smoothly you probably don't pay much attention to the person who's helping you. It's only when you're unhappy or there's some
glitch in the system that the transaction requires you to have more
than a passing interaction. If you keep that in mind, it may be easier for

you to feel some empathy for the other person's position before your interaction turns toxic.

The scenarios that follow are among those most of us deal with most frequently. My hope is that you'll recognize yourself in one or more of these and see how you could use the tools I've given you to change course when you find yourself heading for an impasse.

What Do You Mean I Can't Have My Meds?

Marlene's eight-year-old son, Jamil, was sick with the flu. She'd just come from the doctor, who had phoned a prescription for antibiotics into the pharmacy she used all the time. She'd taken Jamil home, gotten him into bed, and left him with the sitter. Then she'd grabbed her bag, got back in the car, and rushed to the pharmacy, where she'd just have time to pick up the prescription before going to fetch her daughter from soccer practice. She was stressed and not thinking as clearly as she would have if she weren't running late and didn't have a sick child at home.

When she got to the pharmacy Marlene parked the car and practically ran up to the counter, where she fully expected to see Bill, the nice sandy-haired pharmacist with horn-rimmed glasses she usually dealt with. But the man behind the counter was new; Marlene had never seen him before.

It was only when she reached in her purse for her wallet that she realized it wasn't there. She'd taken it out to leave money for the sitter and must have left it on the kitchen counter.

"I'm sorry, ma'am," said the new pharmacist, politely but firmly. "I can't give you the prescription without your insurance card or some form of payment."

That was just one more bit of stress Marlene couldn't deal with. Instead, she flew off the handle. "That's ridiculous," she countered, in effect letting him know she thought he was stupid and incompetent. "I come here all the time and I'll bring the card in tomorrow. Just give me the antibiotics for my son. The doctor said he needs to start taking them today."

But the pharmacist stood firm, repeating that he simply couldn't do what she asked.

Frantic by now, Marlene demanded to speak to the head pharmacist. "I come here all the time," she said again. "Just tell Bill it's me and I know he'll give me the prescription." But his boss wasn't there; he'd already left for the day.

At this point Marlene realized that all she'd been doing was antagonizing the person she needed to help her out. She wasn't giving him any reason to help her and, in fact, was giving him reason not to. So she took a deep breath and apologized. "I'm sorry," she said. "I know you're new here; you don't know me and you're just doing your job. If I were in your place I would have done the same thing. I shouldn't have yelled at you, but my little boy is sick and I'm really worried about him. I'm sure you understand. What would you do if you were in my situation?"

"Well, you could just pay cash for the prescription since you need it right away and you don't have your insurance card," he answered, trying to be helpful.

Marlene nodded. "I know that, and I'd do it if I could, but I don't have my wallet, and my credit and debit cards are in it along with my money and the insurance card. I'd go home and get them, but I'm already late to pick up my daughter from soccer and I'm afraid she'll be getting upset. By the time I could pick her up, get home, and then come back here you'd be closed. So, as I'm sure you can see, I'm really in a bind."

"Well, ma'am, so am I. The pharmacist left me strict instructions not to disturb him unless it was an emergency. And this isn't an emergency."

Biting her tongue and focusing on reflective listening and empathy, she said, "So the bind you're in is that you would like to help me but you can't because you can only call Bill at home if it's an emergency? Is that right?"

"That's about the size of it," he said while tapping away at a computer keyboard, giving Marlene only half his attention.

"Are you worried he'll be mad if you call?" she said, trying to empathize with what she thought he was feeling.

He looked up. "I wouldn't say that, but it *is* only my second day on the job," he said, explicitly denying he was worried while indirectly confirming that he was.

"If I were new here, I would be worried and I wouldn't want to call him." There was an awkward silence during which neither of them seemed to know what to say. Marlene wanted him to ask her whether she thought it would be okay for him to make the call, but he wasn't forthcoming, so she primed the pump. "Would you mind if I tell you what I believe Bill's reaction would be if you called?" He shrugged.

"I think he would be fine with it. Our kids go to the same school, and he's known me and my family for years. I can't imagine he wouldn't want to help me out by taking this one call."

"So you're friends then?"

Being truthful, she said, "Well, we're not close, but we say hello when we meet at school functions and, as I said, I've been coming in here for years. He certainly knows me by name and knows I'm trustworthy."

I like that she didn't stretch the truth by saying she and Bill were friends. By being honest she had credibility, she *acted* trustworthy, which was a lot more meaningful than if she'd said she was friends with his boss. And once she was trustworthy, her opinion of what Bill's reaction might be carried more weight than it had a moment before.

The pharmacist turned from his computer and tore open the bag containing Jamil's prescription, opened the bottle, and shook several capsules into a new pill bottle. "Here's what I can do," he said, handing her the new bottle. "This is one day's dosage. Come back tomorrow with your card and we can give you the rest. This will hold you until then."

Marlene hadn't even thought of this option! By all appearances, the new pharmacist also hadn't thought of it until that moment, or, if he had, was not about to offer it until Marlene had used LEAP.

Marlene had listened, reflected back what she heard, and had not argued with his position, and by doing those things she had discovered the main obstacle standing in the way of her getting what she needed.

When she empathized with his concern—and normalized it by saying that if she were in his shoes she would be worried—she became a friend, if only for that moment. That triggered in him a desire to come up with options for his new "friend."

From that position she was easily able to find areas in which they could agree. They agreed he was in a bind. On the one hand, he was just doing his job and following instructions; on the other, he wanted to help her. This is important, because in the heat of the moment most people assume that the person thwarting them has absolutely no desire to be helpful, which is often not the case. Even though he didn't give her the full prescription or agree with her suggestion to call Bill, she ultimately got exactly what she needed—enough medication so her son could immediately start the course of antibiotics and a quick exit so she could pick up her daughter

THE MECHANIC

Emily was planning to drive to another state to visit her sister, and because she was aware that her car hadn't been running as smoothly as she would like, she took it in for a tune-up so she could make the trip without worrying about having a breakdown on the road. When she picked up the car two days and $865.00 later, she noted she'd been charged for an oil change, an air filter, two new oxygen sensors, and some diagnostic tests she didn't really understand. It looked like the mechanic had done a thorough job, but she'd only gone two miles when she noticed that the engine was still running rough. It was already late on Friday afternoon, she'd had a busy week, and now she was both tired and short-tempered. She immediately turned the car around and headed back to the garage.

"DID YOU ACTUALLY test-drive this car?" were her first words to the surprised mechanic.

He, of course, assured her that he had.

"Well, it certainly doesn't seem that way," she shot back. "The engine is still running rough, which is why I brought the car in here in the first place."

The mechanic, understandably, immediately went on the defensive. He was tired, too, and what he didn't need at the end of a long day was to be dealing with someone who was suggesting he had lied.

"Regardless of what you might think," he said tersely, "I did test-drive your car and it was fine. There's nothing I can do about this now in any case. I'm closing in thirty minutes. You'll have to bring it back end of next week."

Hearing the tone and content of his answer, Emily realized she'd started off in the worst way possible. She had begun to create a toxic argument, and she couldn't afford that because she really needed to have her car fixed before she left on her trip. So she took a deep breath and started over.

"I'm sorry," she said. "I shouldn't have accused you of not test-driving the car. Can you accept my apology?"

"Forget about it," he offered.

Emily then said, "I think it must be an intermittent problem. I hope you can take my word for it when I say it's still not running right. Can you do that?"

The mechanic, who had already been disarmed by Emily's unexpected apology, had no problem agreeing that it must be an intermittent problem, which is why he hadn't noticed it when he test-drove the car, and that the customer had no reason to lie to him about the fact that it still wasn't working properly.

Once they'd found those areas of agreement, Emily asked him another question: "So what do you think is wrong with it?"

"Well, I really did think it was the oxygen sensor, but I guess if it's still running rough there could be something else wrong."

At that point, he began to suggest what that "something else" might be and agreed to go over the car again. Emily then asked if she could pick it up at the end of the next day, which was Saturday.

"I'm really slammed here already," the mechanic replied, "and I already have at least two other cars promised for tomorrow."

Emily reflected back what he'd just told her. But she didn't just repeat what he had said; she looked around at the busy garage, in effect letting the mechanic know she saw what he was up against. "I can see you have a lot to get through. I guess you can't promise it for to-morrow."

"Yeah," he said—looking like he expected her to get angry all over again.

But Emily didn't get angry. "I can appreciate that. I know what it's like when everyone wants you to get their job done right away, especially at the end of the day like this. Sometimes I feel if one more person asks me for something I'll explode!" Her empathic statement was, of course, about feelings of anger, although she never used the actual word.

"You've got that right!" the mechanic said, confirming she had, indeed, guessed his feelings correctly.

"Let me ask you something. I'm leaving on a long road trip on Tuesday and I've got a lot of errands to run before then, so I really need my car back and running properly as quickly as possible. I'd like to continue with you—I think you see the problem—but I'm in a bind here. Is there someone else you could recommend who could fit me in?" (Note that Emily didn't issue a threat: "Well! Then I'll just have to take my business elsewhere!" She was offering a solution.)

"Let me see what I can do," he said as he turned the pages of his grease-stained appointment book.

By keeping her cool, not accusing him of having done a poor job, even giving him an out by suggesting that the problem was probably intermittent and, therefore, difficult to pinpoint, and, finally, by empathizing with his anger, Emily had won over the initially hostile mechanic. Now, instead of wanting to get rid of a nasty, dissatisfied customer, he really wanted to help her out. In the end he agreed to have the car ready for her by the end of the day on Monday and promised to try to get it done sooner if possible.

THE JUNK MAIL WARS—
A TALE FROM THE TRENCHES

This one actually happened to me. I was paying my monthly credit card bill when I noticed a charge from an Internet service provider

I didn't recognize. Since I hadn't ordered the service, I called my credit card company to dispute the charge.

After investigating, the credit card company informed me by mail that the charge was legitimate; the Internet service provider had given them proof that I'd authorized the new service, and I would have to take up the matter with the ISP. I called again and asked them to fax me the "proof," which I was still sure must be bogus. They faxed me a copy of both sides of a check in the amount of $5.00, which was endorsed on the back beneath a line that read, "By signing below, I authorize a monthly charge of $19.95 to be added to my credit card." I recognized the signature as that of my secretary, who has the authority to endorse my checks so she can take care of my banking.

I now knew how this had happened. I get many checks in the mail, and she had undoubtedly endorsed this one along with several others, not noticing that it was actually a junk mail come-on designed to entice customers into buying a new service. I get these checks every day, as I'm sure you do, and, of course, I tear them up, as I'm sure you do, too. But my secretary hadn't torn this one up, and now it appeared I'd be stuck with the charge. I, however, wasn't ready to give up so easily, because when I looked at my previous bills more closely I discovered that the monthly charge had been on my card for six months!

I CALLED THE ISP, and when I got a rep on the phone I immediately explained the situation. "Here's what happened," I said. "My secretary endorsed your check along with a number of others that crossed her desk that day. I understand that's not your problem and that you were legitimately authorized to add that charge to my bill. If I were in your shoes, that's just what I'd be telling me now. But here's my problem. I don't want your service, I won't use it, and I haven't used it to date. I know I can cancel the service, but I'd like to find a way to be reimbursed for the amount I've already paid. So, I'd really like to ask you a favor, if you don't mind."

"Okay, what is that?" asked the rep, who was no doubt relieved to know I wasn't going to accuse the company of charging me illegally but, nevertheless, was still a bit wary.

"Well, if you could put yourself in my shoes for a minute, what would you do if you were me?" That's different from asking him, "What can you do *for* me?" It's actually letting him know I believe he might have information that would be valuable to me. From my experience, I know that when people think they know something you really want to hear, they begin to feel a little bit protective of you. In this case, however, the rep didn't really have any answers.

"Truthfully, I really don't know," is what he said.

"Well," I continued, "has this ever happened before?"

"Yes," sighed the rep. "We get a lot of these calls."

"That must be very frustrating for you," I empathized.

"Yes, it is."

"Okay, then, do you think your supervisor could help us?" Notice that I did not demand to speak to his supervisor, which would have indicated that I didn't think he was competent to handle my problem. Instead, I was once again asking his advice, thereby allowing him to retain some power along with his pride. I also used the word "us" because we had just agreed this situation was a problem for both of us.

"Yes," he said, "he probably could. Can I just put you on hold for a minute?"

I, of course, said that would be fine, and when the rep came back on the line just a couple of minutes later he told me the new service would be canceled as of that day and the money I'd already paid would be credited on my next bill.

This time even I was surprised. The company had been completely in the right; they really didn't owe me a dime, and yet I was getting exactly what I wanted—a refund for a service that I (through my secretary) had actually ordered by mistake. The rep had nothing to gain by doing this for me. When the call ended I would no longer be a customer and I had made it clear I had no intention of becoming a customer because I already had an ISP I was happy with. So why did he do it?

Looking back on it, I have to assume that—because they did, in fact, receive many such calls—the rep was inclined to feel some sympathy for people like myself who had mistakenly ordered the service. But if that were all it took he would have made the offer at the outset. So what caused him to go the extra yard? I believe it was my attention to and respect for the position he was in. Also, the fact that I put my fate in his hands by asking whether he thought talking to the supervisor would help made him feel important. Everyone wants to feel important. And most people want to do the right thing.

How Could You Have Lost My Insurance Claim?

Dale and his wife had been coming to me for couples' therapy. I'd assured them that the majority of my fee for our weekly meetings would be reimbursed by their health insurance provider, and they'd been paying me in full at the end of each session. At the end of the first month, Dale filled out the proper form and submitted it, along with proof of payment, to the insurance company. After waiting a full month without any response, and, incidentally, paying in full for another four sessions, Dale asked for my advice.

Being something of a veteran of the insurance wars, I told him that his claim had undoubtedly been lost and suggested he call the company. He did, and found that they did not, in fact, have any record of his claim. So he resubmitted it, and this time, again on my advice, he kept a copy for his records so that, should they lose it again, he wouldn't have to fill out yet another form.

WHEN DALE AND his wife came into my office at the end of their third month of counseling sessions I could see Dale was seething. He'd waited another month and still hadn't received any response to his resubmitted insurance claim. This time when he called, he was furious. The claims agent had had the nerve to accuse him of not submitting his claim or of sending it to the wrong address. Dale had completely lost his cool, yelling that he had, indeed, sent it, not once but twice, and to the address printed on the form. Then he demanded that the agent allow him to fax a copy of the claim so it would be processed immediately, and the agent had refused.

He'd brought his copy of the form to our meeting, and I suggested that he phone from my office. Before he picked up the phone, however, I told him that, in my experience (and I admit I might be a little paranoid in this instance), insurance claims agents in this particular company were, in effect, working from a script. They were told to say that the client might have forgotten to submit his claim or that he might have misaddressed it. They were certainly not supposed to admit that it might have been lost in their office. By suggesting what might have been the agent's perspective, I gave Dale room to consider that the false accusation wasn't personal.

This time he remained calm when the agent told him he had probably sent the claim to the wrong address. Instead of blowing up at her, he admitted this could have happened (even though he knew it hadn't, it was theoretically a possibility) and asked if he could read her the address to which he'd sent it. Of course, she agreed, and then had to agree that the address he had read to her was, in fact, the correct one.

"So," he said, still remaining calm, "can I ask a favor of you? Would it be all right if I faxed you another copy of my claim? I'd really like to make sure it gets there and that it's processed as quickly as possible."

The agent again refused, saying that accepting a faxed claim would be going against company policy. This time, however, because Dale was not yelling at her, she was not being defensive, just stating the rules.

"Okay," Dale said. "If I understand you correctly, your problem is that you can't accept my fax because that's contrary to company policy. Is that right?"

The agent said that was it exactly, so Dale asked another question. "All right, then, I appreciate your position. So, let me ask you, if you don't mind, I'd like to know—what would you do if you were in my shoes?" He said all this calmly, with no hint of sarcasm in his voice. (Dale went into the call armed with the "What would you do in my shoes" question, which was entirely appropriate in the circumstances. Other questions he could have asked include, "Do you have any advice for me?" and "What would you do next if you were me?" and "What do you think my next step should be?")

Now when the agent said the only thing he could do was resubmit the claim by mail, she sounded a bit apologetic.

Dale agreed to do that, but said he had just one more question, if she didn't mind his asking. She said she didn't, so he asked politely, "What do I do if this happens again?"

There was a brief silence, after which the agent said, "Why don't you just fax it to me," and gave him the number!

Dale was flabbergasted, but when we reviewed the conversation, he was able to see how the dynamic had changed. First of all, he hadn't accused the agent of being wrong or a liar. He'd admitted that he might have sent the form to the wrong address and asked if he could read it to her—even though he was certain he had sent it correctly. She was then able to agree that he had the proper address. The question of whether the insurance company had lost the claim was never mentioned.

Dale then disarmed her further by asking a favor—that he be allowed to fax another copy—and because he was not going on the offensive the clerk didn't need to be defensive when she explained she wasn't allowed to accept claims by fax.

When he asked what she would do in his shoes, Dale was letting her know he really wanted and needed her help—that she was the expert in this situation and he was actually deferring to her greater knowledge.

By that time she had gotten to the point where she was completely nondefensive and actually sympathized with his predicament, so that when he finally asked, "What do I do if this happens again?" she was willing to go the extra yard rather than invoking and enforcing the "rules," and allowed him to do what he had wanted to do in the first place—send a fax. I'd also be willing to bet that, because she felt personally connected to Dale, when the fax arrived it went right to the top of the pile of claims to be processed.

Changing Shoes to Change the Outcome

I asked you at the beginning of this chapter to try putting yourself in the position of the service person who spends his or her entire day fielding calls from dissatisfied customers. If you can manage, just for the length of your interaction, to imagine what it's like to fill those shoes, you'll be in a good position to use LEAP. Don't assume the person has no desire to help you, even if he sounds that way at first. Listen reflectively and identify what his resistance to helping you is. Is it because he's afraid? Is it because you've put him on the defensive? Is it because you are simply a disembodied voice on the phone—not a real flesh-and-blood person he can relate to? Once you understand his position and feelings about it, you can disarm and befriend him. And by doing that you will provide an opening for the other person to try *your* shoes on, effectively stand in your place, and see those things you can agree on—your shared interests. From that point forward options you can partner on—some of which neither of you ever considered—will reveal themselves.

14

LEAP Past Denial

I'm not sick, I don't need help!

—Henry Amador

From alcoholism, anorexia, dementia, and depression to frank psychosis, people who are impaired offer the greatest challenge to those of us who just want them to help themselves. I know from personal as well as professional experience how severely relationships are tested—and sometimes destroyed—because of a person's inability to recognize that he or she is ill. Early in my career I would empathize with clients who were dealing with such a loved one, but I never fully understood their despair and helplessness until I tried to help my brother Henry, who has schizophrenia, a friend with alcoholism, and my mother, who suffered from depression. None of them understood they had a problem, and it was undoubtedly my experience of their denial that propelled me into studying how this psychological mechanism works and how to break through the impasse that's created when someone insists there is nothing wrong with them and they don't need help. I wrote a book on how to break this kind of impasse with people who have schizophrenia and bipolar disorder, so I won't go into those scenarios here. Instead, I will share a personal story about convincing my depressed mother to get help as well as the experiences of three others who used LEAP to break the impasse with people who were unaware of having Alzheimer's, anorexia, and alcoholism.

It's Not in My Head!

Many people have the impression that men are less likely than women to get help for depression. That's true, and it has been confirmed by the research. But the same problem exists for people over the age of sixty-five, who frequently don't recognize that they are suffering from a clinical—rather than normal—depression. Everyone gets blue from time to time, that's normal. But when someone is clinically depressed they suffer from a constellation of five or more symptoms—among the most common symptoms are a sad mood, insomnia, loss of libido, inability to concentrate, weight loss, poor concentration, hopelessness, and sometimes thoughts of death or suicide—that last for a couple of weeks or longer. The disease of depression is hard to recognize in older men and women because it usually manifests in physical symptoms in addition to the ones just mentioned. That confuses patient and doctor alike, sending both off on a wild-goose chase because everyone is convinced the depression is a normal reaction to a physical ailment. That's exactly what happened to my seventy-two-year-old mother.

Maria Cristina had lost more than thirty pounds and suffered from extreme fatigue. She was worried and had been to the doctor virtually once a week over a period of three months. She had no appetite, no energy, couldn't sleep, and felt nauseated and dizzy. I was in New York and she was in Arizona, so I heard about these symptoms over the telephone, but the fear in her voice was unmistakable. She was literally preparing for death. My sister and I talked about her symptoms and began to wonder whether our mother wasn't right to think she was actually near death. According to my sister, she was rail-thin and looked "just terrible." After she was hospitalized for two days for an upper and lower GI series of tests, I decided to go see for myself. Based on the symptoms she described and the fact that all her medical tests were coming up negative for any physical problem, I had begun to suspect she was suffering from a clinical depression.

*   *   *

MARIA CRISTINA WAS a remarkably strong woman. Born and raised in Cuba, she lost nearly everything when she was in her late thirties. Her husband, my father, was killed by the new Castro government, both her parents died of natural causes the same year, and she escaped to America with only her four children. No documents, mementos, or money were allowed on the flight she took to Miami—not even proof of the doctorate degree in education she had earned a decade before. When she landed in America penniless and without proof of her educational status, she started over as a high school Spanish teacher. She remarried and went to night school for seven years to get her second BA, the only diploma she could prove she had.

My mother had good reason to be sad about many things, but she was passionate about life and rarely talked about the past. The woman I knew was not clinically depressed, but this was not the person I saw when I landed in Arizona. Now she could talk about nothing but her past losses and the physical illness her doctors could not diagnose properly. Mostly, she talked about preparing for death.

"Javi," she said, using my family nickname, "I want you to go to the doctor with me tomorrow. I need you to talk with her."

"What about?" I asked.

"About what this thing is that's killing me. Please, Javi." She then burst into tears. I spent most of that first afternoon holding her hand, trying to comfort her, and assuring her that she was not dying.

When I drove her to her appointment the next day, she insisted that the doctor talk with me. We met alone and, as she described my mother's symptoms and the diagnostic possibilities, I became even more convinced this was an episode of major depressive disorder. I asked the doctor if she had recommended a psychiatric consult. To her credit, she had. "But your mother refused," she explained. "She was adamant about it and said she wasn't depressed. 'But Maria,' I told her, 'you look so sad.' But she told me I would be sad too if I had been through what she'd been through and if I were sick. I have to say, that made a lot of sense to me."

It didn't make sense to me, but rather than argue with the doctor, I decided to focus on bringing up the possibility of depression with my mother. When we got home, she made us both *café con leche*, and as we sat at the table sipping our coffee, I said I wanted to talk with her about my conversation with the doctor.

"Mom," I said between sips, "Dr. McElroy told me she asked you to see a psychiatrist. How come you didn't?"

"*Ay, Dios mio!* She is a good girl but sometimes so ignorant. I'm not crazy. Look at how I look! How much weight I've lost, Javi. I can barely walk, I have no energy, and I'm so dizzy! Not you, too!"

"Mom, I'm not telling you you're crazy!" I said, even though I was now convinced she was depressed and desperately needed to see a psychiatrist. "I just wanted to know what happened. Can you tell me?"

"Dr. McElroy said I should maybe take medicine for depression. I don't want this. There's nothing wrong with me."

"So she told you that you maybe needed medicine because she thought you might be depressed? Is that what she said?"

"*Sí*, Javi. Yes."

"You sound mad. Are you?"

"Of course. For three months I am suffering, and because she cannot figure out what is wrong with me, now she says it's all in my head? Look at me! Is this in my head?" she demanded, waving her hands in front of her body.

"No, this is obviously not in your head," I answered, because I agreed with her—clinical depression is not in anyone's head; it is a medical illness like heart disease. "That must have made you lose some confidence in her. You sound very scared. Yes?"

"I am," she said and broke into tears.

The next morning I called her doctor, who knew I was a clinical psychologist and had written a book on depression. In fact, when my mother introduced us she had made a point of reminding the doctor that I was *that* son. So I told Dr. McElroy I was certain my mother had clinical depression. After we reviewed all the symptoms I had seen, she agreed. I asked her if she would be willing to prescribe an antidepressant medication for my mother without getting an independent psychiatric consult. She was more than willing. Later that morning, I sat my mother down with the goal of getting her to accept this prescription from her doctor. I did not need her to acknowledge she was depressed or that she ought to see a psychiatrist. What I needed was for her to be willing to take the medicine. I began by asking her how she'd slept the night before.

"Horrible. I can't sleep at all. How did you sleep?"

"I slept fine, Mom, thanks. But I'm worried about your not sleeping. You can never get better if you don't sleep."

"I know. And I can't eat. I am so nauseous!"

"So when you try to eat you're nauseous?" I asked, to reflect back what she had said and to identify the problems as she defined them.

"Yes, every time."

"What a nightmare. That must make you so worried."

"Yes, yes. Why are you asking about this. You know all this." She looked irritated.

"Sorry. It's just that I got to thinking that maybe Dr. McElroy hasn't been giving you the right medicine."

She brightened immediately—although I am not a medical doctor, my mother was always convinced I knew more about drugs than any other "doctor"—and asked, "What should she be giving me?"

I told her the name of the drug—the antidepressant Dr. McElroy had already agreed to prescribe based on my recommendation—and she scowled.

"That's for depression, isn't it?"

"Yes, but it's not only for depression. Can I tell you what else it's for?"

"Okay. But I don't need a psychiatrist."

"Mom, you don't need a psychiatrist," I reflected back. "I hear you. I am not trying to convince you to see one because I agree you don't need to see one to get better." As it turns out, I was speaking the complete truth. In this instance, she didn't have to see a psychiatrist to get the medicine she needed. "So can I tell you about what else the medicine is for?" I asked.

"Yes."

Focusing only on those problems she herself had described—and depression was not one of them—I said, "It's also to help people to sleep. And I've had patients with gastrointestinal symptoms just like yours who have taken it and gotten better. It's like aspirin. It's good for more than one thing." Again I was speaking the truth.

> I didn't tell her she was depressed. Not once. Nor did I tell her she needed to see a psychiatrist.

"You think I should try it?" she asked, still sounding tentative.

"You really want to know?" I asked, wanting her to feel my opinion would be given only because she asked for it—I was not going to foist it on her.

"Yes."

"I think you should definitely try it. In fact, I spoke with Dr. McElroy this morning and told her my idea. She's in agreement."

"You're a good son, Javi," she said. For some reason, my mother always loved me to speak to her doctors.

Notice that I didn't tell her she was depressed. Not once. Nor did I tell her she needed to see a psychiatrist. Initially, I had desperately wanted her to acknowledge her depression and see a psychiatrist, but when I realized that what I wanted would only lead to an impasse, I focused instead on what I really needed—for her to get the treatment she needed to get better. I made sure I understood and empathized with her experience of the illness and asked as many questions as I could get away with so she would feel respected and in control.

She took the antidepressants and they transformed her. She gained weight, she slept through the night, the nausea disappeared, and she stopped dwelling on the past. The sadness and other physical ailments disappeared as well. For more than a decade, up until she died, she took the medicine. She was engaged in life, in loving her children and grandchildren, and was generally healthy.

Seven years ago, she even agreed to see a psychiatrist! That really shocked me because her own attitudes, the culture she'd grown up in, and perhaps also what she had been through, had made her wary of admitting she had a problem like depression. At first she went because Dr. McElroy had convinced her she needed to see someone who was expert with the medicine. Eventually, although it took many years, she also came to realize she was vulnerable to clinical depression and needed help. Even more surprising, she was open about it and encouraged others to get help. She once gave me permission to speak publicly about her depression, and I know she would be very happy I told her story again here if it could help just one more person.

The Doctors Are Idiots!

Jenny, who was away at college, was close to her mother, Tina, and called her on the telephone every day. During one of these conversations she confided that she feared she was pregnant because she had missed her last two menstrual periods. That didn't make sense to Tina because she knew her daughter practiced safe sex and was not very sexually active. In fact, when Jenny took an over-the-counter pregnancy test, it was negative. When she finally went to see the family doctor during her spring break, she was not happy with his diagnosis.

TINA WAS SLICING onions when Jenny came home from the appointment. She fell into a chair at the kitchen table, sighed heavily, and said, "He's an idiot, Mom. Why do we go to him?"

"Dr. Weber?" Tina asked.

"Yes, Dr. Weber, who else?"

"Why is he an idiot? What did he say?"

"He doesn't think I'm pregnant but he thinks I have an *eating* disorder. I look fine, don't I?" Actually, Tina thought her daughter's face looked drawn and stretched too thin. She couldn't see what her body looked like because Jenny wore baggy clothing and long-sleeved shirts. "I don't know, honey. I can't really tell with the clothes you're wearing, but your face looks different. I've never seen your face this . . . I don't know what to call it, thin, I guess."

"My face looks thin? Oh, come on!" Jenny pulled open the refrigerator and grabbed a bottle of mineral water.

"I'm sorry, but you asked," Tina said, and turned back to slice more onions. "How much do you weigh?" She couldn't help herself.

"Ninety-two pounds. I look fine. If anything, I could lose a few more pounds. Honestly. What a moron he is," Jenny said, standing and walking into the next room.

Tina was now curious, so she did a little Internet research and discovered that her gut reaction to the ninety-two pounds was right. Jenny was more than 20 percent below what would be considered a healthy body weight for a young woman her height. When she caught a glimpse of Jenny coming out of the bathroom one morning with her robe open to reveal what Tina could only describe as skeleton-like legs, her fears were confirmed. Over the next several days she also noticed that Jenny never wanted to eat with the family. She decided to call Dr. Weber.

Some might say it was to his credit while others would call him unethical, but Dr. Weber agreed to talk with Tina about her daughter despite not having Jenny's written consent to do so. He had known Jenny since birth and he was very worried about her. He confirmed his diagnosis of anorexia and added that her blood tests had shown that her electrolytes were way out of balance. What that meant, he explained, was that Jenny's health was seriously compromised. She could even have a heart attack. He told Tina that he had strongly recommended an inpatient treatment program and that Jenny had promised to think about it. She'd also promised to tell her mother.

Tina called her ex-husband, and they agreed that they needed to confront Jenny. While she was still on the phone with him, Tina called upstairs to tell Jenny to pick up the extension.

"Hi, Dad! What's up?" she asked happily.

"The same old, same old, darling. What's up with you?" he asked.

"Like you don't know. Like Mom didn't tell you? I didn't hear Mom hang up. You're still on the line, right?"

"Yes, I'm here and I did tell your father what Dr. Weber said."

"Dad, I'm all right. Mom, I look okay, right?"

"Jen," her father interrupted. "We're both really worried about you. This is serious business. You need to get help. You know that, don't you?" He sounded worried.

"Sure, Dad. I'll do it. Okay? Don't worry, okay?"

"You'll go to the place Dr. Weber recommended?" Tina asked.

"How do you know about that?" Jenny demanded.

"Honey, I was worried after we talked, so I called him."

"Great! Fine! Okay. I'll get help. Bye, Dad. I'll talk to you later." She hung up.

Because Jenny had no insight into the fact that she had anorexia, she understandably never followed through with the referral. From her perspective everyone was overreacting. She was fine.

She promised her mother repeatedly that she would get help but was only buying time until she could return to school. However, only one month after returning to campus she was hospitalized after fainting and hitting her head. While she was in the emergency room, the doctor treating her asked for a psychiatric consult. The psychiatrist confirmed Dr. Weber's diagnosis and the ER doctor's suspicion, and because her health was so precarious, he was able to admit her to a psychiatric unit against her will. But, as he explained to Tina during their first meeting a week later, her daughter was physically stable enough that they would have to release her soon. Tina was terrified because, from her conversations with Jenny that week, it was clear her daughter still didn't believe she had anorexia. The psychiatrist said he wished there was more he could do, but until Jenny admitted she had an eating disorder his hands were tied.

Tina came to one of my LEAP seminars, and when we spoke afterward she told me the story you just read, ending with, "We're at an impasse. She's moved home for the summer. She looks awful, and I'm scared out of my mind. I think I might soon be at the point where I have to try to get her involuntarily admitted to the hospital again."

We talked about whether Tina thought this would help, and she said she didn't. At best, it would be a Band-Aid solution and something she wanted to do only if there were a crisis like the one that had precipitated Jenny's previous admission. She also worried about how her daughter would react to Tina's initiating such a hospitalization. She wanted to try something else before it came to that, which is why she had come to the seminar.

When we talked about how she might use LEAP and, specifically, what she really needed from Jenny, she agreed that, despite what the psychiatrist had told her, she did not need her daughter to say she was sick; what she needed was for her to get better. In this case, she thought the treatment program Dr. Weber had recommended was a bad idea, because the more she learned about it, the more she understood that the people running it would give Jenny the same message the psychiatrist (and to that point her parents) had given her—that she had to admit she had anorexia. And Tina knew from experience that message was going to fall on deaf ears.

She'd found an eating disorders expert through the college Jenny attended and called him and asked some questions I typically recommend to people who are shopping for a therapist. Among the first was, "Given her poor insight, do you think that trying to get her to admit she has anorexia is a good idea?" Because he was trained in motivational interviewing, upon which LEAP is based, the therapist answered no and explained what he would do instead. He would help Jenny find her own reasons to gain weight whether or not she thought she had an eating disorder. Based on what she had heard and also on the college counseling service's glowing recommendation, Tina felt he was the person she wanted her daughter to work with. So her goal—what she needed—was for Jenny to agree to see the therapist when she returned to school in September. Using LEAP, she set out to achieve that goal.

Jenny had just come back from a run when Tina asked her to come into the kitchen so they could talk. Once they were seated together at the table, Tina started the conversation. "Jenny," she said, "I want to talk to you about what happened when you were hospitalized. And I promise I'm not going to try and convince you that you have an eating disorder. Frankly, I don't think we ever need to talk about that again unless you want to. Okay?"

"You serious?"

"Yes. I think there are some other more important things for us to talk about." Tina paused to let that sink in.

"Like?" Tina asked, curious.

"Like going back to school, staying out of the hospital, being happier."

"I'm happy, Mom. You don't have to worry."

"Were you happy when you went to the hospital?"

"Would you be?" Jenny asked.

"No. I would have been furious to be locked up against my will and have people tell me I had a problem I don't have," Tina said, reflecting back the things her daughter had told her months before while she was still in the hospital and empathizing with the emotions Jenny had expressed.

"Thanks. I was furious," Jenny said.

"Anyone would have been."

"So you think they made a mistake?" Jenny asked, confusing her mother's reflective listening and empathy with agreement.

"What I think doesn't matter. I'll tell you if you want to know, but, honestly, what you think is what rules the day. Right?"

"I guess it does at that," Jenny said, smiling.

Having successfully delayed giving her opinion, and having disarmed and befriended her daughter, Tina went straight for their areas of agreement. "I think staying out of the hospital is a goal we can both agree on. Am I correct?"

"Sure. But that will never happen again," Jenny stated confidently.

Tina asked her how she could be so sure, and Jenny naïvely said she just knew it, that was all. Rather than confront her naïveté, Tina then asked Jenny to talk about why she thought she'd ended up in the hospital in the first place.

"Well, if I hadn't passed out and hit my head, none of this would have happened," Jenny replied.

"So, if you didn't pass out and hit your head, you wouldn't have been admitted to the hospital? I would have to agree with that. But can I ask you something?"

"What?"

"A lot of people end up going to emergency rooms every day in situations similar to yours, but not many of them end up being admitted to a psychiatric ward against their will. Why do you think that happened?"

"That damned ER doctor is why!"

Tina acted genuinely curious about this answer and the ones that followed. It was easier than she thought it would be because this was the first time she'd actually been aware of her daughter's thought process regarding the hospitalization, and it was fascinating as well as disturbing. She realized that Jenny was ignoring many of the details of the event and that the gaps in her knowledge were what made much of her denial possible.

Tina wanted to see if she could help her daughter fill in some of those gaps—examine some things she hadn't looked at before because she was too busy defending herself against the "false" accusation that she had anorexia. So she asked her, with genuine respect for her opinion, whether not only the ER doctor but also the consulting psychiatrist, her inpatient treating psychiatrists, the nurses, and other staff could all have it wrong. She did this in an authentically curious manner, and what Jenny ultimately came to, entirely on her own, was this. She still thought they had the diagnosis wrong, but she had to admit that her being thinner than most people, along with her low blood pressure—which is why she'd blacked out—her electrolyte imbalances, and her missed periods could have fooled them all into making the wrong diagnosis.

"I must have a supersensitive system so that when I lose a little weight everything goes out of whack. But, Mom, I saw some of the other girls in there with real eating disorders. They had tubes up their noses because they were being force-fed! I'm not that bad," she said.

"No, you're not," Tina agreed, then asked, "But it sounds like you can see why the doctors all made a mistake in your case. Is that what you're saying?"

"So you think they made a mistake?" Jenny asked hopefully.

Feeling she had delayed long enough and that the timing was right, Tina asked, "Do you really want to know what I think?"

"Yes."

Remembering to use the A tools, she said, "Well, I'll start by apologizing because what I'm going to say may be disappointing and make you mad at me. But I could be wrong," she quickly added to help Jenny save face. "I hope we can agree to disagree. But, yes, I think it adds up to an eating disorder, although it's clearly not as bad as the other girls you saw."

"I thought you saw my side of it," Jenny said, looking disappointed.

"I think I do see your side of it, at least I hope I do, just not on this one issue. But who cares if I'm right or you're right? I don't ever want to argue about that again. It seems like what matters most is that you don't end up with the doctors making the same mistake again. Right?"

"Exactly right."

"So what can you do to keep that from happening?"

Starting with their area of agreement—that the combination of Jenny's imbalanced electrolytes, low blood pressure, missed periods, and the relatively low weight that was causing these symptoms had convinced the doctors and nurses she had anorexia—they then talked about a plan they could partner on. That's when Tina told Jenny about the eating disorders specialist she'd talked to up at her school. She quickly added, "This counselor told me he doesn't care whether the two of you agree you have a disorder. He even said he wouldn't want to talk about that if you didn't think you had one. He said it would be pointless."

"That's crazy. What would he want to talk about then? It doesn't make sense."

"Well, he knows a lot about healthy diets and these symptoms that are concerning the doctors. He could help you choose a target weight you felt good about that would also fix your other problems. If you could do that, I think you'd avoid this whole eating disorder issue altogether. He told me he would work with you on *your* goals."

> "I never imagined that by avoiding the whole question of anorexia, by not telling her she was wrong when she said she didn't have it, I could help her to do something about it!"

Jenny saw the counselor when she returned to school, and now, two years later, as of this writing, she is still in treatment with him. She has regained some weight and, over time, she has come to call the disorder her "metabolic weight problem." As far as I know she still thinks she never had full-blown anorexia. And who cares? Tina said it best: "I never imagined that by avoiding the whole question of anorexia, by not telling her she was wrong when she said she didn't have it, I could help her to do something about it!"

By giving her daughter respect and not dismissing her opinion, Tina's opinion started to matter more to Jenny. And because Tina's opinion about what Jenny should do was based on what Jenny herself wanted, it was an easy sell.

WHERE ARE MY KEYS?

Three years ago Gerald was diagnosed with Alzheimer's disease. He did not yet need around-the-clock nursing care, but he did need someone to keep a close eye on him, which his wife of thirty years was happy to do. But she needed a break. Their daughter, Melinda, offered to stay with her father for a week while her mother was away on vacation. Although she knew her father had a lot of trouble remembering things, she hadn't realized how much trouble this would create when she was trying to care for him. Power struggles were daily events. She wrote to me about two of these instances because she wanted me to know how much LEAP had helped her to help her father. I asked to interview her for this book, and here is what she described.

MELINDA'S DAD WAS banging around in the kitchen and cursing. She went to him and asked him what was the matter. Bent over, both hands yanking silverware out of the drawer, he said, "Dag-nabit! I can't find my keys!"

"What keys are you looking for?" Melinda asked.

"My car keys! Why aren't they in here? I always leave them here! Do you know where they are?" She did. She also knew he had not been allowed to drive for almost two years.

"Dad, maybe you forgot, but you know you aren't allowed to drive anymore."

"What in the Sam Hill are you talking about? I was driving twenty years before you were even born."

"Yes, Dad, I know. But you've got Alzheimer's. You haven't driven in a long time now because you forget things."

"What are you talking about? I can drive."

"Not anymore, Dad. I'm sorry," Melinda said, at which point Gerald started calling upstairs to his wife. He asked Melinda to go get her, and when she tried to explain that her mother was away, he said that was nonsense and started looking for his keys again.

Melinda hated to see her father so upset. Realizing they were at an impasse and things could easily get worse if she kept trying to convince him she was right, Melinda remembered LEAP. "Dad, are you looking for your keys in there?" she asked.

"Yes. Have you seen them?"

"I haven't seen them," she said, which was technically true, because her mother kept them in her purse. "Can I ask you something?"

"What?" he said, still rummaging through the drawer.

"Can you look at me for a second?" Melinda asked in order to help him focus.

He stopped rummaging then and looked up, seeming bewildered and a little scared. Melinda felt a tight knot swell in her chest as she said, "Can I ask where you want to go?"

"You just did."

"So I did," she agreed, feeling as if she'd been caught with her hand in the cookie jar. "So where *do* you want to go?"

"We need milk and eggs."

"So you want to drive to the store to get us some milk and eggs?"

"That's right."

Softly, she said, "How frustrating that you can't find your keys."

"It is, sweetie. It is very frustrating."

"I'd be frustrated, too, Dad. I'm sorry."

"That's okay," he said, sounding much calmer.

"Have you looked in the refrigerator?"

"For the keys?!" he asked, eyebrows arched and smiling.

"No! That was silly of me. Sorry. I meant let's see if maybe we have some milk and eggs." Not waiting for an answer, she opened the door and there, in plain sight, were a dozen eggs and a gallon of milk.

"Oh. *There* they are. I guess I forgot," Gerald said, sounding perplexed and a little defeated.

"I forget things all the time. It's frustrating," Melinda commiserated. "Come on, let's watch some TV."

Gerald shrugged and followed her into the family room.

MELINDA DESCRIBED A second instance when she was able to use reflective listening along with the empathy, agreement, and partnering tools. Her father kept wanting to talk to his wife. He kept forgetting she was away. "Where is she?" he would ask, and Melinda would say she was in Florida visiting her sister.

When she did this on one occasion, Gerald became suspicious. Scowling at her, he said, "She would never go to Sally's without me. What are you not telling me?"

"Dad, I'm telling you the truth. She's in Florida."

"Then why can't I talk to her? Why are you keeping me from talking to her?" Melinda's gut reaction was to defend herself—he had just spoken to his wife that morning—but she knew that would only result in an "I'm right, you're wrong" argument, and further upset her father. So instead she reflected back what he had just said: "You want to talk to Mom and I'm keeping you from doing that. Is that right?"

"Ahh! So you admit it. Why would you do that?"

"Dad, I didn't admit or deny anything. I just wanted to be sure I was understanding what you were saying. So you're wondering why I would keep you from talking to Mom. Is that right?" she asked.

"I do wonder. Is she in the hospital? Is she okay?" he asked, worried now.

"She's fine," Melinda said, careful to not mention Aunt Sally again because her father didn't believe his wife was there. "You sound a little worried that I'm lying to you. Are you?"

> She did a great job of letting go of the need to be right and butt heads. Moreover, she was able to reduce his anxiety by joining with his anger and suspicion.

"Well, I don't know if you're lying or not. But why can't I talk to your mother?!" In fact, Melinda was trying to stall him because he'd called three times the day before and her mother had started to worry that she should come home. Melinda had convinced her to stay but didn't think she could keep winning that argument if he continued to call three times a day. So she set her sights on what she needed, to calm her father down and gain his trust so he wouldn't keep calling. She said, "I swear she's okay, Dad. Can you trust me on that?"

"I suppose. But why can't I talk to her?"

"Dad, it's your right to speak to Mom, and I'm not going to stop you. That would be disrespectful. Right?" she asked, underscoring their areas of likely agreement.

"That's right."

"Good, because—"

"So get her on the phone. I can talk to her, right?"

"You can, but she's very, very busy right now and it would be better if we could talk to her later."

"Why? What's she doing?"

"I'm not sure," Melinda answered truthfully, "but I know she needs not to be disturbed right now and I promise I'll get her on the phone after dinner. Can we agree to that?"

"I suppose, but I don't like it."

"I wouldn't like it either, but I am glad you trust me, Dad. We'll call after dinner, okay?"

"All right."

What was so powerful about Melinda's approach was that she frequently acknowledged her father's perspective and feelings without ever offering her opinion. She did a great job of letting go of the need to be right and butt heads. Moreover, she was able to reduce his anxiety by joining with his anger and suspicion. And she was able to gain his trust, which ultimately led to the plan they partnered on—calling after dinner. As it turns out he didn't bring the issue up again after dinner. Either he forgot or let it go because he felt less anxious.

I'm Not an Alcoholic!

Raphael and Gary, both thirty-four years old, had been close friends since they were children. They spoke almost every day and saw each other at least once a week. Gary had been best man at Raphael's wedding. Now Raphael felt certain that Gary had a drinking problem, and he was worried about his friend. Ironically, he came to this conclusion based more on what Gary had told him than what he had seen firsthand—not that he hadn't seen some things with his own eyes that gave him pause. The irony was that the most damning evidence came from Gary's own lips, and yet Gary didn't think he had a problem. He was characteristically defensive the very first time Raphael raised the issue.

THEY WERE SITTING at a bar, watching a basketball game and waiting for their food to arrive. Gary had just ordered his third whisky; Raphael hadn't finished half of his first beer. "So, check this out," Gary said, raising his empty tumbler for one last try at sucking whisky from the ice. "Sunday night I stopped off at that new bar on Ninety-second and it was a scene! You have to check it out. I mean, it was a Sunday night and the place was packed." Shaking his head, quietly laughing, he said, "Oh-oh, ma-an, I got so plowed I didn't make it to work the next day!"

"Ouch!" Raphael said in sympathy. "Isn't that the third time this summer you called in sick?"

"Yeah, but so what? It's summer and you only live once."

Knowing that this seemed to happen about once a month regardless of the season and that Gary's girlfriend had broken up with him because of his drinking, Raphael said tentatively, "You know, maybe you should watch your drinking."

"What the fu . . . ?! Are you going to jump on that wagon, too?"

"Hey, don't put me in the same boat as your ex. I was just saying—"

"You were just saying I'm an alcoholic. Just like her. And I have the same answer for you. Read my lips. *I am not an alcoholic!*"

Although he had not actually used that word, Raphael had, in fact, come to the conclusion that his friend was an alcoholic. Gary had been telling more and more stories about people who, as he put it, "gave him a hard time" about his drinking. And he described certain events that seemed to prove them right. He'd even been counseled by the human resources director at his job for drinking too much at a recent company convention. Gary's answer to that was, "Everyone drinks at those meetings!" He didn't say what Raphael was thinking—*but not everyone gets called to HR afterward.* His doctor was also giving him a "hard time" because his blood pressure and weight were up and he was advising Gary to either stop drinking or cut back drastically (Gary had told the doctor he drank every night, usually between three and eight or nine drinks). Around the same time, he'd been arrested on a DUI. Hearing these stories peppered with Gary's lame explanations and laughter sealed it for Raphael. The only question was what to do about it.

He'd tried ignoring the problem and, thereby, the conflict that trying to talk about it would have created. He'd hoped that Gary would come to the realization on his own, but the problem seemed to be getting worse. Now Raphael found himself missing his friend even when they did get together, because Gary could only talk about the people who were giving him a hard time, while at the same time he drank to the point of pontificating without pause and slurring his words.

> "Don't ever tell him he has a drinking problem unless he drags your opinion kicking and screaming out of you."

Raphael had started to avoid him, but when he spoke to his wife about the situation, she encouraged him to talk to Gary again, this time using LEAP. She had been to one of my seminars and thought Raphael was in the best position to at least get Gary to stop being so defensive and think about how much he was drinking. She told Raphael about reflective listening, strategic empathy, the three As, and the "golden rule," as she put it: "Don't ever tell him he has a drinking problem unless he drags your opinion kicking and screaming out of you." Raphael thought it made sense and wanted to try it out, but not in a bar or any other setting where Gary was likely to drink a lot. He invited Gary to go on a hike the following Saturday.

Harriman State Park is only one hour from New York City but light-years away in terms of the sweetness of the air, the expanse of lush green forest, and the sounds of rushing mountain streams. After nearly two hours spent hiking uphill, Gary and Raphael reached the peak that was their goal. When they sat down and unpacked their lunch, Raphael was disappointed to see Gary pull out a flask. "Want a hit?" he asked Raphael.

"No, thanks," his friend replied. As they ate, they talked, and Raphael looked for an opening. It came when Gary said, "I met with that defense lawyer yesterday."

"Yeah? What did he say?"

"He said that although this was a first offense, the blood alcohol level was going to be a problem. They're going to suspend my license and fine me for sure, and there's a real possibility of two weeks in jail."

"What was your blood level?"

"Let's just say it was really high."

"How are you feeling about this lawyer?"

"I think he's a straight shooter."

"Are you nervous?"

"Yeah. I mean, I need my car to get to work. And if they send me to jail for two weeks I'm going to lose my job. I can't tell them about this."

"Why not?"

"They wrote me up after the convention, and there was another time I didn't tell you about."

"What other time?"

"I came to a meeting late one morning; I'd been out drinking until probably four in the morning. I mean, I didn't set out to drink that late but one thing led to another. Anyway, they said they could smell alcohol on me. Maybe I was sweating it, I don't know, because I brushed my teeth and used mouthwash. I know a lot of people who drink as much as I do. I don't know why I have to be the one to get caught."

"Why didn't you tell me about that?"

"I didn't want you giving me a hard time. I didn't need to hear you tell me I'm an alcoholic."

Raphael wanted to reflect this back because he knew it was the part of Gary's experience he needed to join with. So he said, "You didn't tell me because you thought I would give you a hard time and call you an alcoholic?"

"Yeah. So are you going to start lecturing me?"

"I'll tell you what I think if you like, but I'd rather be clear on what I'm hearing first. Can I ask you another question?"

"Sure."

"What do you think?"

"About me being an alcoholic?"

"Yeah."

"I'm not. You remember my old man. Now that was an alcoholic. He passed out drunk every night, and his liver gave out on him when he was fifty. That's not me."

"What you're saying is you're nothing like your father, who was obviously an alcoholic. You're not an alcoholic. Right?"

"Yeah. That's right. I'm nothing like him," Gary said, looking down at the ground.

"Then it must really piss you off when someone says you're an alcoholic. I mean, I know you hated that about your father."

"Yeah, it does piss me off. So what do you think?"

"I don't like the term, so I'm not going to use it. But what I'm about to say might piss you off anyway. I hope not, and if it does I'm sorry. I don't know everything, Gar, and I could be wrong. But it seems to me that your drinking is causing you some big problems. Wouldn't you agree with that?"

"Guess I would have to when you put it that way."

"You ever try to cut back? I mean, like after you got nailed that second time at work?"

"Yeah. But I couldn't do it. I tried, you know? I promised myself no more drinking on weeknights, but that lasted exactly one day. It was depressing."

"What about getting help?"

"You mean AA? No way!" Gary laughed. "I'm not standing up in some crummy church cellar with a bunch of drunks clutching Styrofoam cups of coffee in their shaking hands and saying, 'Hi, my name is Gary and I'm an alcoholic.' I mean, I know it helps a lot of people, but those people are bona fide alcoholics. That's not for me."

"You're the one who mentioned AA, not me. I just meant help in general. I didn't even know you were trying to cut down. You could talk to me about it. Maybe see a counselor who isn't going to tell you to quit. You know, just someone to help you cut down."

What his friend did for Gary was priceless. Others had tried unsuccessfully to convince him he was an alcoholic. They inadvertently were keeping him at an impasse. This conversation was the first time Gary had ever been honest with another person about not having control over his drinking. Raphael was able to lower Gary's defenses, redefine the problem in terms Gary himself would accept, and help his friend start to think about his drinking and the negative impact it was having on his life. Before this conversation Gary only defended his drinking, which interfered with his ability to reflect on it. Raphael gave him the space to really reflect. Where this led, ultimately, was that when his DUI case went to court, Gary agreed to counseling in exchange for no jail time.

He also became more open with Raphael and others about his own concerns about his drinking. With more openness came more insight and personal accountability. That was the key to his starting to work on the problem for the first time in his life. After that one conversation it was not unusual for Raphael to ask, "How's the drinking going?" and for Gary to tell him without any defensiveness what goals he had, or had not, met that particular week.

Anyone familiar with the research on recovery from alcoholism will tell you that this form of insight, together with a desire to make a plan to cut back and a willingness to do it publicly (by being honest with friends and a therapist), bodes well for recovery.

IN EACH OF the scenarios above and in the preceding chapters, the door was open, if only a tiny bit, to talking about the impasse. But what if one of you has slammed the door shut? What if, because of anger, defensiveness, or negative expectations, the person refuses to talk with you about the issue? In these situations the LEAP tools you have learned can be applied, along with some new ones, to open closed doors.

15

LEAP Through Closed Doors

Obstacles are those frightful things you see when you take your eyes off your goal.

—Henry Ford

Often, when I give a talk or lead a seminar, someone will tell me that he or she thinks it's too late. There is no longer any relationship at all between him and the loved one with whom he'd been in conflict. In fact, they haven't spoken in weeks, months, or even years. There's too much water under the bridge.

The good news is that it's almost never too late. Even if your loved one is angry at you, distrustful, and avoiding you altogether, you can usually still get back the relationship you've lost. And if you can let go of your desire for control—the need to prove that you're right and the other person is wrong—you can reopen the door to getting what you needed in the first place. Opening a line of communication and immediately disarming and reassuring the person is the first step.

Speak Friend

If you've read the book or seen the movie *The Lord of the Rings*, you may remember the scene in which Frodo and Gandalf are standing outside the Mines of Moria, desperate to enter. The stone door is shut tight against them. Over it, carved in stone, is the inscription "Speak Friend." For hours Gandalf puzzles through the meaning of those words until Frodo asks him, "What is the Elvish word for friend?" and when he answers, the gate finally opens.

If the door to dialogue is locked, the key that will open it is finding a way for the person on the other side to experience you as a friend so that he will feel it is safe to reengage in conversation with you. I have to assume he's experienced you in this way before, so you do have a foundation on which to rebuild, but if he now refuses even to hear you, how can you do that?

What You Should Say to Open the Door

Saying the word "friend" in Elvish isn't going to do the trick. Even if it would work, if the person isn't picking up the phone you can't say anything. Generally, what I suggest people do in such instances is to write a letter or an e-mail. First of all, if the person won't talk to you, what other options do you have? But, beyond that, correspondence is nonthreatening. It can be read in privacy and considered at leisure. And the recipient doesn't have to worry about what your reaction to his reading it will be. It's safe.

So, what do you write? First, remind the person that you love and miss him and then use the three As. Say that:

- you're sorry for what has gone before;
- you might have been wrong—you don't know everything;
- you respect the other person's point of view (something you clearly have not done in the past) and that if he agrees to speak with you, you promise not ever to tell him he's wrong again.

What you don't want to say is that you wish the other person would have done such and such. Don't blame him for his reaction to you and under no circumstances mention your position again. Instead, stay focused on the apology, express your fallibility, and make the promise to not preach or otherwise push your point of view. Ask that you agree to disagree.

Larry had not talked to his daughter Jessie in almost a year. They had argued bitterly over her decision to move across the country. During that argument he told her she was young, foolish, and would live to regret her decision. He also cut her off financially, refusing to participate in what he unfortunately had called "stupidity." All three Es that mark a toxic argument were evident in spades. In addition to the name-calling (she was naïve and foolish) he would kitchen-sink it, reminding her of every bad decision she had ever made in her life—instances in which he was right and she was proven wrong. But worse than this pattern of escalation was the evasion and entropy that ensued. After she moved, Jessie refused to return her father's phone calls or letters. Her mother implored her to speak with her father but Jessie was resolute. Larry still thought the move was a terrible idea but realized that more than anything he missed his daughter. And besides, without a line of communication he would never convince her to move closer to home. So he wrote the following letter:

> Dear Jess,
>   I cannot tell you how sorry I am for being so hard on you about moving. Perhaps I was wrong about that. I don't know it all. Your mother tells me you're happy there and doing well. Please trust that if you will talk to me again I promise to never again bring up this issue. I can respect your decision to move and won't try and convince you to come back home. I miss you very much.
>   All my love,
>   Dad

Jessie called Larry the day she received the letter.

Whether you do this in a letter or in person, it will usually open the door. Remember Roberta and her fourteen-year-old daughter, Amanda? They were having the battle over bedtime and Amanda's late-night messaging. Roberta had slapped her daughter after Amanda called her a bitch, and Amanda had been giving her the silent treatment ever since. When she was forced to answer her mother, she simply yessed Roberta and did whatever she wanted (like staying up past her bedtime to message her friends). They were at an impasse and their relationship was suffering horribly. Roberta used the tools I have described here to re-open the discussion with her daughter. Here is how she described their conversation:

"I am sorry I slapped you. That was wrong," Roberta began.

"I'm sorry I called you a bitch," Amanda quickly answered. "Can I go now?"

"Not yet. I also want to say I'm sorry for not listening to you. I want to talk about your bedtime again and I—"

"I don't want to talk about it. I get it! I'm in bed by eleven, okay?"

"Not really. I want to talk about this in a different way. I don't think I've really been listening to your point of view, I just keep telling you you're wrong, it's a school night, I'm your mother, I know best, blah, blah, blah." Roberta was particularly proud of the "blah, blah, blah" because she felt she was really in Amanda's skin when she said it, and after she said it Amanda smiled just a bit. "Amanda," she went on, "I really am sorry and I really do want to hear you out."

"That's okay, Mom. We don't need to talk about it," Amanda said, still trying to avoid the discussion. But Roberta was ready with an important promise.

"Wait a second, please. I have one more thing to say, and then you can talk about it or not. I will leave it up to you. Okay?"

"I guess so."

"If you'll talk with me about this, I promise I will just listen. I won't use anything you say against you and I won't tell you you're wrong to think what you think."

"So you're saying I can go to bed later?"

"No. Not yet. First I really want to hear your perspective and I promise I won't tell you you're wrong or irresponsible or anything like that. Can you just tell me again why you want to stay up and why it's not hurting your schoolwork?"

As you already know, that apology and promise worked to open up the discussion and led to Roberta's being able to break through the impasse.

Showing respect for the other person's perspective as Roberta did is a cornerstone of using LEAP. If you've failed to do that in your arguments with someone and the door has been slammed shut as a result, you can use it now to reopen the dialogue.

> Many people balk at the idea they should promise never to volunteer their opinion again, but when reminded about how many times they've told the other person he's wrong in the past, and what the outcome has been, they see the wisdom of this advice.

One thing you need to understand, however, is that the other person may find it difficult to believe you've suddenly done such an about-face, and the best way you have to reassure him is to make the promise that you will never again thrust your opinion in his face unless and until he asks for it. Explain your reasoning. You can say something like, "I've tried to convince you before and I've never been able to do it. Our relationship is more important to me than convincing you I was right." And empower the person by saying, "And if I slip and do give you my opinion again, I won't blame you for shutting me out." The goal here is to make it safe for him to talk with you again and to make transparent your genuine change of heart—you no longer care about being right.

Many people balk at the idea they should promise never to volunteer their opinion again, but when reminded about how many times they've told the other person he's wrong in the past, and what the outcome has been, they see the wisdom of this advice. So if you, too, are resistant to the idea of making such a promise, think about that. And also think about the fact that the other person is already quite familiar with your opinion and isn't likely to forget it, whether you repeat it or not. If you want, if it makes you feel better, you can even say you're not sure you'll be able to keep that promise, but you're going to try. That's honest, it expresses your true desire to respect the other person's point of view, and it models fallibility. If you can say you're not perfect, it becomes easier for the other person to admit the same.

In any case, you already know that ideally you should never give your opinion unless it's requested, and when you use LEAP that will happen, even if you have to prompt the other person by asking his permission: "Hey, can I tell you what I think?" Once he's had enough experience of you behaving as a friend, he will certainly say, "Sure, go ahead." So the fact is that, despite your promise, you *will* have the chance to give your opinion again, but with more power than you had before—especially if the other person was refusing to speak to you at all.

WHEN BUSINESS IS A FAMILY MATTER

Brad and Jeff are brothers who were in business together. Brad had loaned Jeff several thousand dollars that he assumed Jeff would repay. Jeff, however, believed he had satisfied his debt by doing a particular job that took a significant number of hours and that they would otherwise have had to hire an outside contractor to do. Neither one of the brothers was willing even to consider the other's point of view, and, in the end, Brad simply told Jeff flat-out that he was deluding himself by thinking he'd repaid the loan and that so far as Brad was concerned, his brother was stealing from him. He couldn't, didn't, wouldn't for a moment respect Jeff's point of view and the result was that, by the time I met Brad, the brothers hadn't spoken to one another for more than a year.

IT WAS BAD enough that these two men who truly did love one another and who had been working together were now feuding, but, to make matters worse, their estrangement had affected the entire family. They refused to attend family functions together and were both being put under extreme pressure by their family members to mend their fences.

After explaining the fundamentals of LEAP to Brad, I recommended that he write Jeff a letter like the one described above. I explained that by apologizing and indicating that he could have been wrong, he would not only be returning the locus of control to his brother but would also be modeling some flexibility in his thinking and thereby making it likely he would get the same in return because, as I explain below, people tend to return such personal gifts in kind. And finally, by saying you could be wrong, you allow the other person to save face. This is very important, because when people are defending their pride and self-respect, there is no room for rapprochement.

> Brad, of course, still wanted his money, but his first goal was to mend his relationship with Jeff.

It has been well documented in social psychology that when we give someone a gift, he or she will likely give a gift of similar or even greater value in return. If we reveal something intimate about ourselves, for example, the other person will reveal something of similar personal value. Perhaps this principle explains some of the attraction many feel, despite not always acting in this way, to the axiom "It is better to give than to receive." So what Brad wrote his brother was, "I'm really sorry. I feel as if I've never listened to you. All I've done is accuse you, and I'm sorry for that. Maybe I've been wrong about this. All I know is that I miss you, I miss our family's being together, and I would like to fix that."

Then came the promise: "I really would like to get together with you and talk about this, and I promise I will never again tell you that you owe me the money. You will never hear that from me again unless you ask." Brad, of course, still wanted his money, but his first goal was to mend his relationship with Jeff. Their feud had put a strain on the entire family, and he really did love and miss his brother. And the fact was that, if they weren't speaking, there wasn't much chance he'd get his money back in any case.

He sent his letter in the form of an e-mail and received one in return saying that Jeff was willing to meet with him. The meeting was very emotional, and it was clear the estrangement had been difficult for both of them.

Because I'd been working with Brad—role-playing their conversation and coaching him on how to use the delaying tool to avoid giving his opinion—he was very good about keeping his promise. And, ultimately, the brothers were able to have a fruitful conversation about what boiled down to an unfortunate miscommunication. They both regretted what had happened between them and they were both willing to take some of the responsibility. Jeff said he might not have been clear about the fact that he believed he was repaying his debt by doing extra work, and Brad began to see that he might have had a reason to think that. In the end, Jeff did actually repay a significant portion of the money. An impasse that had lasted a year and taken a significant emotional toll was resolved in the course of a week.

WHEN GOOD INTENTIONS GO AWRY

If it's so easy for two fundamentally reasonable, rational people like Brad and Jeff to argue themselves into an apparently irreconcilable impasse, it's that much more difficult to repair the damage when one of the parties has other problems as well.

It was Peter's drinking that drove a wedge between him and his parents. They could see it was ruining his life, and for years they had been nagging and badgering him to get help, get therapy, go into rehab. But Peter steadfastly maintained that he didn't have a problem and could cut down on his drinking whenever he wanted. Except that he apparently didn't want to.

FINALLY, PETER'S WIFE couldn't take it anymore. She insisted that he leave the house and was granted custody of their young son, Joey. By the age of thirty-five Peter was living a marginal existence and sinking deeper and deeper into his alcoholism. Then one day Joey, who was by now twelve, went to visit his father, letting himself in, as he always did, with a key. On this particular afternoon, however, he discovered Peter passed out on the floor and was unable to rouse him. In a panic, Joey called 911 and then phoned his grandparents—he didn't want to call his mother because he knew she would be furious. Peter's parents went immediately to the emergency room, where they told the doctor their son had been talking about taking his own life. They wanted him to stay in the hospital, they wanted him to get the help he so badly needed, and they knew he'd never check himself in voluntarily. The only way to ensure that he'd be committed for at least three days was to lie and say he'd told them he was going to commit suicide. They hated to lie but they desperately wanted to help their son, and they genuinely feared he might kill himself, if only inadvertently.

Peter was, of course, released at the end of the holding period, and from that day on he wouldn't even talk to his parents. To make matters worse, his ex-wife then obtained a court order allowing him only supervised visits with Joey, which resulted in his having far less contact with his son. He was now almost completely cut off from his entire family.

Peter's mother came to see me because she still feared for her son's life, and she knew that so long as he wouldn't even speak to her or her husband there was nothing they could do to help him. She still felt that, at the time, she had done the right thing for both her son and her grandson, and she knew that if the same situation recurred, she'd do it all over again. But when, at my suggestion, she called Peter, she didn't tell him that. Instead, she apologized with humility, saying she could have been wrong and maybe she'd made a mistake. She then stated her purpose in calling, which was that she really missed her son and wanted them to be able to interact with one another again. And she made the all-important promise that she would never again complain or even talk about his drinking unless he asked her or if it was a matter of life or death.

Peter did agree to talk to her again, and when they did she discovered that what had upset him the most was that his son had stopped speaking to him and he'd lost his visitation rights. He wanted those things back. Whereas previously his parents had been so busy arguing with him about whether he had a drinking problem that they'd never even talked about Joey, they were now able to agree with him that, for both their sakes, Peter's relationship with his son needed to be mended. And Peter was able to agree that the only way to accomplish that was for him to go into rehab (even though he still didn't think he had a drinking problem).

When You're the One Who Walks Out

In the previous two situations it was the person who'd had the door slammed in his (or her) face who ultimately found a way to reopen it. But what if you're the one who walked away? You may regret your impulsive behavior, regret even more the loss of a friend or a loved one, and want to get back what you've lost.

That was the situation with Annette and Brenda, close friends for many years, who got into an argument, and ultimately an impasse, when Annette took it upon herself to give Brenda advice about her love life. Most people don't want to hear what you have to say "for their own good," and until they're good and ready, you're not going to convince them they're making a big mistake.

BRENDA HAD BEEN dating a married man, and, initially, Annette supported the relationship because Brenda assured her that her lover was seeking a divorce. After a couple of months, however, when there was no evidence that he was getting any closer to becoming a "free man," Annette started to grow suspicious and convinced Brenda to ask him point-blank, "Exactly how far along are you in your divorce proceedings?"

When she did just that, Brenda was shocked to learn that not only had he not filed for divorce, but he hadn't even told his wife of his intention to do so. "I was leaning hard in that direction," was his only explanation. "I'm really sorry if there was some confusion." When Annette heard that, she told Brenda she really needed to break off the relationship—and not just for her own good. "How would you feel if you were that man's poor wife?" she asked. But what Brenda heard was that Annette was calling her a home wrecker. That quite naturally put her on the defensive, and she retorted by reminding her friend of the time when she'd been going through a rough patch in her own marriage and had gone out on a dinner date with another man.

Annette, however, had salvaged her marriage and had never actually had the affair she'd been contemplating. She was taken aback and deeply offended by Brenda's counterattack, didn't see that the situations were in any way comparable, and responded by storming out of Brenda's apartment and slamming the door behind her.

Back home and somewhat calmer, she could see why Brenda had felt the need to defend her own behavior by attacking Annette's, and she regretted her behavior. So she picked up the phone and called to apologize. "I'm sorry I walked out on you like that. It was rude."

"It was more than rude. It was insulting," Brenda said.

"You feel I insulted you?" Annette reflected back.

"Yes. You made me out to be a whore and a home wrecker. I don't appreciate that."

"I wouldn't appreciate it either. I am so sorry."

"Why did you say that anyway? Why would you?"

"It must have hurt your feelings. Did it?" she empathized while ignoring the question.

"Yes, it did," Brenda said, sounding calmer. "So why would you say such a thing? Do you actually believe that about me?"

"Do you really want to know?" Annette asked, making her friend responsible for whether she really wanted to hear her opinion again.

"Yes, I do."

Using two of the A tools, Annette said, "Well, again, I'm sorry that this might feel hurtful and I hope we can agree to disagree about it, but all I was really saying was that I felt bad for his wife and that I know if you weren't directly involved in the situation you would feel bad for her, too."

During the long pause that followed Annette felt tense, but she needn't have, because finally Brenda said, "You're right. I do feel terrible about it."

In the course of their conversation they made peace with one another, and Brenda began to talk some more about her feelings for the man she was involved with and the situation she was in. As she talked, and Annette didn't argue with her, she gradually talked herself into seeing that this was not a healthy relationship and that it wasn't getting her any closer to her real desire, which was to start a family of her own. All Annette had to do was listen and empathize. She didn't have to present her own opinion because she'd already said her piece.

LEAP Through the Door
Before It Slams

Ideally, of course, you want to find a way out of your impasse before the door to resolution has slammed and locked, leaving you out in the cold. That's the point a couple I know had reached with their teenage daughter when we met for dinner one night. Danielle had broken her twelve o'clock curfew and her parents had told her that since she'd proved herself to be so irresponsible, from then on she'd have to be home by nine. Not surprisingly, Danielle was furious and had gone into full-blown sullen, sulking teenage mode. She hadn't spoken to her parents for three days, and it didn't seem to them that there was any end to this behavior in sight. In fact, they were starting to get angry with her all over again.

When I suggested to Danielle's parents that they apologize to her, they, in turn, suggested that I must have just lost my mind. But I explained that I wasn't telling them to say they were wrong. "You do think you're right, don't you?" I asked. Of course they did. Well, then, I said, you need to get comfortable with that, and you don't need to convince Danielle of your rightness just now. What you need to do is convince her that you respect her opinion, which is that her breaking curfew was no big deal and she should still be allowed to stay out until midnight. Why can't you do that? What have you got to lose? You do, after all, have the power to get her to do what you want anyway, and you do feel certain of your opinion.

> The apology opens doors because it is a way to convey respect for the other person's views and feelings. And when people feel respected, they are more apt to give.

But my friends couldn't see it that way. They said they were afraid Danielle would get confused and think they were changing their minds about her new curfew. "But you're not going to say that, are you?" I asked. No, of course they weren't.

It took more conversation to get them to understand my point, but in the end they did apologize, and when she was once more speaking to them they learned that Danielle wasn't actually as angry about her new curfew as she was about her parents' having refused to listen to her point of view. In fact, the main complaint among many of the teenagers I've worked with is that their parents don't listen to them. The apology opens doors because it is a way to convey respect for the other person's views and feelings. And when people feel respected, they are more apt to give. In this instance the gift Danielle gave her parents was letting go of her anger and the silent treatment she had been giving them.

CONCLUSION

LEAP in Life

Real success is not on the stage; but off the stage as a human being, and how you get along with your fellow man.

—Sammy Davis, Jr.

As I've said all along, learning to listen, empathize, agree with the person with whom you're arguing, and look for ways to partner with him gives you much more than a way to deal productively with arguments that have turned toxic and stalled. LEAP provides the tools you can use to better your relationships with loved ones, business associates, even complete strangers. It is a way of relating to people that is inherently satisfying and yields positive results every time. In the end, even if you fall short of breaking the impasse, the positive result may be as simple as feeling good about yourself for not getting bent out of shape—feeling proud that you didn't take the bait and get sucked into an argument. Or it may offer an unforeseen gift, as it has for me many times. Let me give you a recent example of what I mean.

In New York City parking is at a premium, and at parking meters a quarter buys you only ten minutes. It's a quarter well spent, however, as tickets are typically more than one hundred dollars! On one particular occasion, I parked at a meter and discovered that I had only one quarter in my pocket. Instead of ducking into the nearest bodega to get change, which would have been sensible, I fed the meter my single quarter and rushed down the street to do my errand. Ten minutes later, or perhaps it was eleven or twelve, I was walking back to my car when I saw a parking violations agent standing there and writing me a ticket. I was furious. I thought she was wrong to give me that ticket since I couldn't have been more than one or two minutes late. Was she just hovering like a vulture waiting for the moment the meter clicked "Expired"?

I stopped walking toward the scene of the crime—as far as I was concerned she, not I, was the criminal—and stood still for a moment to consider my options. I knew I was going to get the ticket. I have a lot of confidence in my ability to be persuasive, but I knew there was nothing on earth I could say to stop a New York City parking violations agent who was halfway through writing a ticket. So, however much I wanted her not to give me a ticket, I had to accept the fact that I was too late for that.

What was left then?

What I needed was to not feel so upset and powerless. Anger is generally a good thing; it can direct us in ways that are helpful, but in this instance it would serve no purpose except to ruin what was left of my afternoon. I felt victimized—as silly as that sounds—and I didn't want to feel that way. The quickest way for me to let go of my anger and maybe regain some sense of control was to find a way to connect with this person. In a strange way it became a challenge. I didn't want her to coldly place the ticket under my windshield wiper. I wanted to make a connection. This was no small task I had set for myself. If you've ever gotten a ticket in New York City you know that most agents won't even make eye contact, much less talk to you. I believe they're trained to do this in the same way I was taught as a boy never to look a snarling dog in the eye. Just act calm, ignore him, and walk away. Do that and you won't get bitten.

I considered her perspective, stepped forward, and simply said, "Hello."

As I could have predicted, she didn't look up. It was as if no one had spoken to her. Although I'm not a mind reader, I had a picture of what she was probably feeling because I have seen parking violations agents take a heap of abuse. I have personally seen them cursed at, screamed at, and even, on one occasion, kicked. It is a thankless job. Instead of the kind of greeting I had given, they are generally on the receiving end of comments like, "I was gone for one minute! What the hell is wrong with you! This isn't fair. Come on, this is bullshit and you know it!" and far worse. So her ignoring my politely delivered greeting didn't surprise or upset me.

The next thing I said was, "I am not going to argue with you. I was wrong to let the meter run out. I really was just saying hello."

She looked up then, still doubtful and no doubt waiting for me to ask her to stop writing the ticket. So I said, "I am not going to ask you to not give me the ticket. Like I said, I know you're just doing your job. I shouldn't have let the meter run out."

She looked up again, shaking her head now, and said, "The meter wasn't the only thing you let run out." She pointed with her pen to the stickers on my windshield. "Your registration and inspection are also expired."

"No way!" I said, genuinely surprised.

"Both of them, just last week," she confirmed.

As I stepped closer to see for myself, I laughed and said, "What a moron I am! I do this kind of thing all the time. I deserve three tickets; then maybe I'll remember the next time they're due."

Now, I can't say I know for certain that she was thinking these things about me, but by focusing on what I imagined her perspective to be—which came naturally once I'd decided to connect with her—I was a lot closer to her point of view than I would have been if I'd told her I didn't deserve any of those tickets. What happened next, even though I have seen things like this happen countless times when I embrace another person's perspective, seemed like pure magic. She looked me in the eye and said, "You're not a moron, you just forgot."

"Yeah, but we're not just talking about the meter. I forgot the registration and inspection, too!"

"They're only a week overdue," she said again.

When she handed me the ticket—that's right, it was just one ticket rather than three—she said with mock severity, "I didn't write you up for the expirations because I know you'll take care of them right away." Then she smiled and winked before turning and walking away.

It may sound strange, but in that moment I felt a great deal of affection—maybe even a kind of love—for that woman. Not because of the tickets she didn't write but for what she had given me—a little bit of herself—when she dropped her defenses, listened to what I had to say, and smiled. And it didn't hurt that she also saved me a couple of hundred dollars.

Learning LEAP is really about paying attention, being mindful of whether you are too defensive or angry to have a productive interaction with another person. If you are, you will do damage every time. In the little example above, I could have gotten into my car, slammed the door, dealt with a pounding heart for the next twenty minutes, then revisited the whole experience when I got home and had to write a check for the ticket. Instead, I felt happy when I got behind the wheel, and when I wrote my check later that night, I smiled and enjoyed retelling the story to a loved one. But as important as teaching you to be mindful of your own feelings is that LEAP also teaches you about the power of being curious about and respecting another person's experience. When you do that, you can transform any adversary into a teammate. And together you can usually find a mutually satisfying way to move forward.

So remember to strap on your tool belt in the morning. When you disagree with someone, don't be afraid to stop giving your opinion and start listening. Become curious about the other person's perspective and what he or she wants. When you use these tools and the others LEAP provides, you will not only be able to break almost any impasse, you will also find that your relationships become more meaningful.

One final but very important thought I want to share is this: The reason LEAP has worked for so many people in so many situations is that it focuses on relationships, not outcomes. With healthy, respectful, and trusting relationships, no impasse is impenetrable. So keep your eye on the prize—the relationship. I have a Post-it on the wall I face whenever I write. Like LEAP, it helps me to do that by asking: "What really matters to you?"